KT-549-646

British Politics
A Beginner's Guide

Bromley Libraries

30128 80246 802 8

ONEWORLD BEGINNER'S GUIDES combine an original, inventive, and engaging approach with expert analysis on subjects ranging from art and history to religion and politics, and everything in-between. Innovative and affordable, books in the series are perfect for anyone curious about the way the world works and the big ideas of our time.

aesthetics
africa
american politics
anarchism
ancient philosophy
animal behaviour
anthropology
anti-capitalism
aquinas
archaeology
art
artificial intelligence
the baha'i faith
the beat generation
the bible
biodiversity
bioterror & biowarfare
the brain
british politics
the Buddha
cancer
censorship
christianity
civil liberties
classical music
climate change
cloning
the cold war
conservation
crimes against humanity
criminal psychology
critical thinking
the crusades
daoism
democracy
descartes
dewey
dyslexia
economics

energy
engineering
the english civil wars
the enlightenment
epistemology
ethics
the european union
evolution
evolutionary psychology
existentialism
fair trade
feminism
forensic science
french literature
the french revolution
genetics
global terrorism
hinduism
history
the history of medicine
history of science
homer
humanism
huxley
international relations
iran
islamic philosophy
the islamic veil
journalism
judaism
lacan
life in the universe
literary theory
machiavelli
mafia & organized crime
magic
marx
medieval philosophy
the middle east

modern slavery
NATO
the new testament
nietzsche
nineteenth-century art
the northern ireland conflict
nutrition
oil
opera
the palestine–israeli conflict
parapsychology
particle physics
paul
philosophy
philosophy of mind
philosophy of religion
philosophy of science
planet earth
postmodernism
psychology
quantum physics
the qur'an
racism
rawls
reductionism
religion
renaissance art
the roman empire
the russian revolution
shakespeare
shi'i islam
the small arms trade
sufism
the torah
the united nations
the victorians
volcanoes
the world trade organization
world war II

British Politics
A Beginner's Guide

Richard S. Grayson

ONEWORLD

A Oneworld Book

First published in North America, Great Britain and Australia by
Oneworld Publications, 2010
This revised edition published 2016

Copyright © Richard S. Grayson 2010, 2016

The moral right of Richard S. Grayson to be identified
as the Author of this work has been asserted by him in accordance
with the Copyright, Designs and Patents Act 1988

All rights reserved
Copyright under Berne Convention
A CIP record for this title is available from the British Library

ISBN 978–1–78074–878–8
eBook ISBN 978–1–78074–968–6

Typeset by Jayvee, Trivandrum, India
Printed and bound by Clays Ltd, St Ives plc

Oneworld Publications
10 Bloomsbury Street
London, WC1B 3SR
England

Stay up to date with the latest books,
special offers, and exclusive content from
Oneworld with our monthly newsletter

Sign up on our website
www.oneworld-publications.com

Contents

Acknowledgements

I would like to thank all the students I have taught since the mid-1990s. Their challenges to me have made a major contribution to my thinking on the broad subject of British politics and I am grateful to them all.

A note on terminology

The United Kingdom covers Great Britain (England, Scotland and Wales) and Northern Ireland. As is commonly the case, this book uses 'Britain' and 'British politics' as a shorthand for matters relating to the entire UK.

1

Introduction

Two election results in 2015 illustrated that British politics is an unpredictable business with the public and parties capable of confounding the 'experts'. In the 2015 general election, the vast bulk of political pundits had expected there to be no overall majority, with most predicting Labour as the largest party. David Cameron's return to power as leader of a Conservative majority prompted much questioning of the accuracy of opinion polls, just as John Major's surprise victory in 1992 had done. Four months later, there was a bigger shock in the Labour Party. Ed Miliband had resigned as party leader immediately after the general election and a contest to replace him took place. At the start of the party's leadership election, Jeremy Corbyn had odds of 100-1 and they would rise to 200-1. Yet he swept to victory in a manner which is causing many to re-examine what they thought they knew about British politics and its likely direction in the years to come. There is now a serious discussion about left-wing politics in Britain, which has not been held since the 1980s, and much of that is because of Corbyn's leadership of the Labour Party.

These 2015 shocks came at the end of what *The Times* had called on 13 May 2010 'a very British revolution': the coalition government of Conservatives and Liberal Democrats established following the general election held a week before. Before the 2010 election, no Liberal had sat in the Cabinet since 1945, when the wartime coalition ended. The UK's electoral system is stacked very much in favour of one party having an overall majority, and the 'hung parliament' which led to a coalition has only occurred once in recent decades 1974, when a coalition was not the result. Most remarkable of all was that the Liberal Democrats sat in coalition with the Conservatives. Such a deal stuck in the throats of many members of both parties due to their long-standing ideological hostility to each other. Many pundits predicted that the coalition would not last a full five-year term. Yet it did so, with not a single Cabinet-level spat resulting in resignations. What did happen at its end, though, as many predicted, was the virtual annihilation of the Liberal Democrats, in parliamentary terms, in the 2015 election. They went down from 6.8 million votes and 57 MPs to 2.4 million votes and just 8 MPs. Meanwhile, a new force had emerged: the Scottish National Party, led by Nicola Sturgeon. It had hoped to win independence for Scotland in the 2014 referendum. It failed to do so, but the energy that ballot created saw it claim 56 of Scotland's 59 seats, mostly at Labour's expense, and emerge as the third largest party in the House of Commons. Simultaneously, although Nigel Farage's United Kingdom Independence Party (UKIP) won only one seat, in gaining 3.8 million votes it could claim to be the UK's third party in terms of vote share.

The changes which took place over the 2010–15 period, since the first edition of this book, pose big questions in British politics. Can an overtly left-wing political agenda ever achieve political success in Britain? Is there a future for the Liberal Democrats? How will Scotland's place in the world develop? Has UKIP peaked? Is UK politics the victim of cyclical political hegemony, where one party repeatedly dominates Westminster elections? This book places these questions in the context of some deeper and long-running issues in British politics in the hope that it will help readers make sense of the often confusing rituals of Parliament, and tackle the growing belief that many people have of politics being pointless.

It is written partly from the perspective of someone who

has been strongly involved in politics since the 1980s – for the Liberal Democrats for 25 years, before joining the Labour Party in 2013. But as a university lecturer in British politics, I also had the chance to stand back from the day-to-day process and to reflect on why, for so many people, British politics is so mystifying, frustrating and often just downright annoying.

In the final analysis, it is society that produces its politicians. That partly means that if a society is obsessed with celebrities, then politicians will put themselves forward as personalities. The most mundane aspects of their daily lives become public property because that is what the public is interested in. The media tells us so much about the wives of party leaders because the public is genuinely interested in them, just as much as or more so than it has an interest in party policy. We saw much of that during the 2010 campaign, and for all that Nick Clegg very effectively argued for his party's policies, the 'Cleggmania' which followed the leaders' debates on TV can partly be understood in the context of a celebrity-obsessed culture. More recently, this may explain the appeal of Boris Johnson and Nigel Farage, and in a curious way, the avowedly anti-personality politician Jeremy Corbyn.

Society's influence on politics is not seen only in the froth of election coverage. It is also seen in the limits on politicians' actions. For example, there are regularly local public campaigns against politicians apparently callously wanting to close local schools. But more often than not, these decisions are not driven by what politicians want or do not want to do. Rather, they are driven by population factors such as birth rates. In the 1980s, schools which had flourished as the 'baby boomers' went through school in the 1950s and 1960s became unsustainable due to there being fewer children. The Conservatives took much flak for school closures, but they were largely beyond the control of government. The vast range of social changes which have taken place in Britain in recent decades are well beyond the scope of this book. But they need to be stated at the outset as huge constraints on what politicians can achieve.

One central question runs through this book: why should we care about British politics? That is a question increasingly on the minds of a public that tends to assume some or all of the following:

- It makes little difference which party is in power because they are all generally the same.
- Politicians promise much but deliver little, and sometimes know that they can deliver little even when they make promises.
- Politicians generally serve their own interests and/or the interests of a small group of people, which might be, for example, their party, a business, a profession, or a union.

Related to that broad 'Why should we care?' question are several other pressing contemporary issues.

Is British politics in crisis? That question is crucial given the rise in public cynicism about politics and politicians. At the same time, in spite of occasional waves of enthusiasm for a specific leader, political parties find it increasingly hard to recruit members and activists. That is not necessarily because people are any less 'political', but because they choose to direct their political activities into single-issue campaigns and pressure groups. If that trend continues, can the current structures maintain themselves? In short, will there be anyone left to govern?

What is Britain's place in the world? Britain's proud or shameful (depending on your perspective) imperial past has left it with a sense of being a world player. Yet it is now not even entirely sovereign over its own affairs, due to membership of the European Union, let alone the affairs of others. How influential is Britain now, and how do other countries influence us?

Have all political parties become too similar? Parties are often the most mysterious part of the political process. This book addresses what really makes them tick and how people get involved, examining whether we really need parties.

Who has real power in politics? Throughout the book, the roles of different government institutions and the power of personalities are considered. Who really is making the decisions? As a background to that, the influence of the media, sometimes difficult to quantify, is assessed.

Does British politics work? There are two aspects to this subject. First, the book explores the mechanisms of politics so that readers can gain a better understanding of how the institutions of the state have evolved. For example, how does a policy contained in an election manifesto become enacted as law? Second, it considers whether these processes actually do a good job. As we will see, the answer to the question of whether the system 'works' depends on your values and what you want to achieve.

I hope that anyone reading this book might get to its end and be at least a little less cynical about the political process. I believe that most politicians genuinely do have ideals and that they set out on a political career with the best intentions. Moreover, it is argued that political parties have (at times, though not always) made a significant impact on the direction of government policy in ways that have affected the lives of everyone in the country. Above all, the author hopes that people who read this book might realise that they can make a difference if they get involved in politics and will choose to do so.

2

'Events, dear boy, events': a brief history of British domestic politics since 1945

Today's British politics begins in 1945. Although that may seem long past, we are still living with the legacy of the kind of welfare state set up by the Labour government of 1945–51. Its institutions and systems are fundamentally still in operation today. Ever since then, politicians have been trying to make them work, not least because the National Health Service remains dear to the hearts of the British people. The other reason for taking 1945 as a starting point is that the characters and events of the years since then are central to the intellectual hinterland of most of those (journalists and academics) who comment on politics today. There is a great propensity in Britain to look at the past as a guide to the future, and much political comment is littered with references to how Attlee handled his Cabinet, or how Callaghan tried to deal with the unions. So it is essential to have some idea of the history if one is to understand the comparisons that are drawn between it and politics today. This chapter includes some of the unexpected events that caused problems for politicians and which led Harold Macmillan to say, 'Events, dear boy, events' when asked by a journalist about the most challenging problems facing governments. Although policies do play a part in the chapter, it is not policy focused. Rather, policy is used to illustrate general points about the nature of governments, with details being left for the chapter devoted to policy.

1945–51: creating the modern welfare state

The welfare state was not suddenly established in 1945. Even prior to the First World War, the Liberal Party had laid the foundations of the welfare system with provision for some pensions and unemployment benefits. This system had been steadily developed in the inter-war years, with all parties playing a role. Neville Chamberlain as health minister was especially active in expanding healthcare provision. By 1939, Britain had one of the world's more developed welfare systems.

However, the Second World War brought about a revolution in the way people thought about welfare provision. This was partly due to the practical demands of war. The Luftwaffe's bombs paid no attention to the ability of their victims to pay for hospital treatment and the Emergency Hospital Scheme was established at the outbreak of war to provide free treatment for the civilian wounded. Meanwhile, the Emergency Medical Service coordinated the work of previously disparate hospitals. Such measures can be seen as the basis of the National Health Service in that they proved that such coordination was possible.

Aside from practical developments, there was also an ideological shift in 1939–45. As Paul Addison's classic book, *The Road to 1945* (1975), sets out, the shared experience of war encouraged people to embrace collective ways of tackling shared problems. This had an impact on government at the highest levels. As early as 1940, government decided that it was not only necessary but desirable to tackle the problems the country faced in a collective manner, not only during the war but after it. Its War Aims Committee agreed in August 1940 that it would:

consider means of perpetuating the national unity achieved in this country during the war through a social and economic structure designed to secure equality of opportunity and service among all classes of the community.[1]

This was exceptionally radical language for 1940 and committed the government to pursuing the kind of agenda which both Labour and the Liberals, but not the Conservatives, had favoured prior to the war. A result of this aim was the publication of the *Report of the Inter-Departmental Committee on Social Insurance and Allied Services* in late 1942. Known for short as the *Beveridge Report* after its chairman, the Liberal academic William Beveridge, the report proposed a national system of benefits (including pensions) financed by insurance contributions from workers, employers and state. Beveridge's aim was to tackle five 'giants' which he said stalked the land: want, disease, ignorance, squalor and idleness. His scheme to do this would be supported by a safety-net system of 'public assistance' for those who had not been able to make contributions to the main insurance scheme. Beveridge also said that, to be effective, this system would need to be underpinned by a National Health Service, tax-financed family benefits and state action on unemployment. He did not go into detail on these, but set out a clear direction.

The report was massively popular with the public, but the Conservative Chancellor of the Exchequer, Kingsley Wood, saw it as far too radical. Consequently, plans were made for how the scheme could be implemented, but a decision over whether or not to do so was put off until after the war. For the remainder of the conflict, Labour campaigned for 'Beveridge Now', by which they meant that the proposals of the report should take effect immediately. That message had a significant positive impact on Labour's popularity. None of that is to say that all Conservatives were opposed to post-war social reform. Indeed, the establishment of a new secondary-school structure was pushed through by a Conservative, R. A. 'Rab' Butler, in the Education Act of 1944. However, when it came to the 1945 general election, Labour was best placed to capture the new mood. Even though he had led Britain to victory, Winston Churchill was not seen as the best choice for post-war Prime Minister and Labour won by a landslide.

LABOUR'S JULY 1945 LANDSLIDE			
	Seats	Votes (no.)	Votes (%)
Conservative	213	9,988,306	39.8
Labour	393	11,995,152	47.8
Liberal	12	2,248,226	9.0
Others	22	854,294	2.8
Turnout: 72.8%			

The Labour Party that won in 1945 had never secured a majority at any previous election. Yet it was full of experienced ministers. Many had served since 1940 as members of the coalition government set up in that year. The new Prime Minister, Clement Attlee, had been deputy PM to Churchill, while others such as Herbert Morrison and Ernest Bevin had played crucial wartime roles. Attlee was a very different character to Churchill and was no great rhetorician. But he led an extremely talented Cabinet and was a highly effective coordinator of those talents. He certainly needed to be, as the tensions between some of his ministers were great. One well-known story tells how, within Bevin's earshot, someone remarked that Morrison was his own worst enemy. Bevin retorted, 'Not while I'm alive he ain't.'[2]

Despite these rivalries, and the fact that the ministers had endured five years of wartime government, the Attlee governments of 1945–51 (punctuated by an election in 1950) were energetic and radical. In welfare, the Beveridge Report was implemented through the National Insurance Act (1946) and National Assistance Act (1948). Aneurin 'Nye' Bevan pushed through the National Health Service Act in 1946 against stiff opposition from the British Medical Association, whose members (doctors) resented being taken over by the state. When the NHS came into existence in 1948, it was the world's most advanced health system providing free treatment for all.

The war had left a severe housing problem in many bomb-damaged cities. When combined with the terrible conditions of pre-war slums, this meant that housing was a pressing issue for any government which wanted to better the day-to-day lives of the people. Labour sought to tackle the problem by building a million new homes by 1951. Many of these were in New Towns around London, which gave people the ability not only to get out of polluted cities, but enjoy quick access to the country-side. Meanwhile, the collective spirit was also applied to many industries. The government nationalised coal, gas and electricity production, the iron and steel industry, and inland transport (most notably the railways). This was based on a view that these areas of the economy were so crucial to the nation that they should be run by government in the interests of all. Moreover, all except iron and steel were loss-making and there was little argument from anyone about the need to keep such failing industries going for the nation as a whole, even if there was a cost to the taxpayer.

The Labour Party could feel satisfied about implementing so many socialist measures, but it faced severe economic difficulties while it did so. The national finances (and therefore Labour's welfare policies) rested on an American loan of over £1 billion. This had a very generous interest rate of two percent and annual repayments were not to begin until 1951. In addition, the UK received generous payments under the Marshall Plan, the US scheme for helping to boost post-war economies in Europe. However, as a condition of the loan, the US had insisted that the

British pound should be convertible to the dollar by 1947 as a measure to encourage global trade. Yet the British economy was so weak that convertibility went badly wrong and trading in the pound was suspended. In late 1947, a series of cuts in spending and increases in taxation were introduced by the Chancellor, Stafford Cripps, initiating what became known as the 'Age of Austerity'. The atmosphere of gloom had already been worsened by a terrible winter in early 1947 during which fuel stocks failed to keep pace with demand. Meanwhile, although the war was over, much rationing continued until at least 1948. Indeed, bread had never been rationed during the war but was in 1946–8.

GREAT PRIME MINISTERS – CLEMENT ATTLEE

The policies of Clement Attlee (1883–1967) dominated British politics until the 1970s and defined the era of post-war consensus. He was seen by many as an unlikely political leader. Churchill is widely held to have described him as a 'sheep in sheep's clothing' although there has never been any proven source for that. Yet he led Labour into a majority government for the first time on the basis of two election victories, and the National Health Service his government built remains one of the most treasured institutions of British society.

The basis of Attlee's success was his ability to offer clear direction while at the same time dealing with the massive competing egos – such as Ernest Bevin, Nye Bevan and Herbert Morrison – in his own Cabinet. Attlee effectively managed the Cabinet, resolving differences between colleagues. Sometimes he did that through compromise and sometimes through clear direction, but it was always evident that he was in charge. Moreover, there were some issues on which he led from the front, most notably on Indian independence, which was a long-standing personal political passion for him.

GREAT PRIME MINISTERS – CLEMENT ATTLEE (cont.)

His terse style was crucial to this. On one occasion in September 1947, Attlee faced dissatisfaction over his leadership and was visited by Cabinet minister Stafford Cripps, who told him that he should stand down so that Bevin could take over, and that Bevin had agreed to this. While Cripps sat in his office, Attlee phoned up Bevin and said, 'Ernie, Stafford's here. He says you want my job.' Bevin said he didn't and Attlee replied, 'Thought not', and won Cripps over by offering him a promotion.[3] Such economy of style, and also understanding of how to butter up Cabinet colleagues, illustrates how Attlee dealt with the many challenges he faced: face up to the issue, deal with it and move on. He was brilliant at it.

The 1945–51 period also saw significant developments in Britain's role in the world (which are discussed further in Chapter 8). The most damaging of these for Labour's domestic policy was engagement in the Korean War of 1950–2. The costs of this were one factor which put pressure on government spending and led to the introduction of prescription charges. A general air of austerity led to the government becoming unpopular in the late 1940s and its majority was slashed in 1950. When a tired Clement Attlee, struggling to maintain a majority in Parliament, called an election in 1951 in a desperate bid to win more seats and shore up his position in Westminster, his gamble failed and the Conservatives were the beneficiaries.

1951–70: Butskellism and consensus

The Conservatives, initially led by Winston Churchill, were to remain in government for the next thirteen years. Ironically, they benefited from Labour's economic policies, which may have been unpopular at the time, but had laid the foundations for economic growth in the 1950s. Labour had kept inflation low, had increased industrial production overall, and had boosted Britain's success in global trade with exports rising much more than imports.

The Conservatives built on much else that Labour had done in 1945–51. They had opposed the establishment of the NHS, arguing that its structure was over-centralised. But they had not opposed the principle of a free-to-use national system, and soon came to terms with the existence of the NHS. Moreover, they had become enthusiastic about other aspects of Labour policy and in 1951 pledged to build more houses than Labour had done. As regards nationalisation, they sought only to unpick some aspects of Labour's radical measures: the road haulage aspects of inland transport and, crucially, the iron and steel industry, which was denationalised in 1953 (only to be renationalised by Labour in 1967). The extent to which the Conservatives had accepted Labour's post-war settlement is perhaps best seen in the response of Churchill to the 1954 rail strike. The PM felt that railway workers' demands for higher pay were justified and directed British Railways to agree to the demands, even though that would mean operating at a loss and making further demands on the national budget. Meanwhile, *The Economist* looked at the similar policies pursued by the outgoing Labour Chancellor (Hugh Gaitskell) and the incoming Conservative Chancellor (Rab Butler) and said that it did not matter which party was in power because 'Mr Butskell' remained as Chancellor.[4]

The idea of 'Butskellism' has influenced much academic writing on the 1951–70 period, which is usually seen as a time of political 'consensus' even though there were changes of both the Prime Minister and party at the country's helm. A dominant theme of writing on post-war politics, especially associated with the work of Dennis Kavanagh, one of the most respected academic experts on the post-war years, is that the Labour and Conservative parties (the Liberals were still small in the 1950s and 1960s) pursued similar policies in government. The consensus defined by Kavanagh and others can be seen as having five principal characteristics.[5] First of all, governments were committed to maintaining full employment. None of them believed that it would be right to return to the mass unemployment of the 1930s. Many politicians of all parties had become politically conscious in that decade and regarded the unemployment they saw as morally wrong. That applied just as much to Conservatives such as Harold Macmillan and Edward Heath as it did to Labour leaders. Second, they saw an extensive role for government in running a mixed economy, hence disputes over the scope but not the principle of nationalisation. Third, they were committed to high levels of welfare spending. Fourth, they were committed to conciliating trades unions. Finally, these attitudes were underpinned by optimism that active government, reinforced by the expertise of the civil service, could tackle most challenges which came its way.

This approach to the 1950s and 1960s has been challenged by some writers, who argue that profound differences existed between the parties, and that even when they pursued policies, they were doing so to achieve different ends.[6] Much work now focuses on particular areas of policy in an effort to see how much agreement there really was on specific issues.[7] Arguably, most writers accept the basic idea of consensus, while recognising that party disputes continued.[8] So what becomes interesting about British politics in the 1950s and 1960s is establishing exactly where and why there were differences of opinion.

GREAT PARTY LEADERS – HUGH GAITSKELL

The people remembered as the greatest leaders in British politics tend to be Prime Ministers. Yet leadership is often seen in its rawest form in opposition parties. Unsupported by the power of office and the vast resources of tax-funded Prime Ministerial offices, there have been several examples of politicians who have made a significant impact on the shape of British politics without ever themselves being in a position to hold the highest office.

Hugh Gaitskell (1906–63) was the first avowed Labour moderniser in the party, believing that the party was too left-wing to gain power and that it must change if it was ever to win. Like Attlee, he did not come from the party's working-class roots, yet he was passionate about social justice and believed that the Labour Party needed to make this a priority. However, he felt that the party put off middle-class voters with its economic policies, and argued that this needed to change. He fought unsuccessfully to change Clause IV of the Party's constitution, which dictated support for greater nationalisation. However, he ultimately won arguments over the need for the UK to maintain a nuclear deterrent – which many saw as a test of Labour's commitment to a strong defence policy. Seen by many as a leader of great energy, he died suddenly in early 1963 and it fell to Harold Wilson to lead the next Labour government.

MOVERS AND SHAKERS – TONY CROSLAND

Tony Crosland (1918–77) was the most important thinker of post-war Labour politics. Although Crosland held high office (Foreign Secretary in 1976–7), and was very influential as Secretary of State for Education and Science in 1965–7 (see p. 125), he was most important because of a book: *The Future of Socialism* (1956). It was in some way accidental that this book was ever written. First elected to Parliament in 1950, Crosland lost his seat in 1955, and

MOVERS AND SHAKERS –
TONY CROSLAND (*cont.*)

having previously been an academic (after wartime membership of the Parachute Regiment), he returned to writing. Despite its title, the book he wrote was more about social democracy than socialism, arguing that the Labour Party needed to change to adapt to modern circumstances, embracing aspects of capitalism it had once opposed, while passionately pursuing a more egalitarian society. The book offered intellectual underpinnings to Gaitskell's project to change the Labour Party and had a huge impact on the centre left more widely. A line runs directly from Gaitskell to Blair, Brown and New Labour. There is also a link between Croslandite thought and that of the Liberal Democrats. Few British politicians have written a book as influential as Crosland's, which can well be described as the most influential British political text of the post-war years.

Undoubtedly, the biggest single dispute between parties was the Suez crisis of 1956. The details of this are discussed in Chapter 8, but Britain's role in it gave the Labour opposition (and the handful of Liberals) a big stick with which to beat the government. It brought to an end the political career of Anthony Eden, who cited 'ill health' as his reason for resigning as PM in 1957 to be replaced by Harold Macmillan. A further dispute between parties was over 'sleaze' (a term generally in use from the 1940s to indicate corruption and/or scandal in politics), as seems to be so often the case when a party has been in power for many years. The specific point at issue towards the end of the long period of Conservative rule was the relationship between the married Secretary of State for War, John Profumo, and call girl Christine Keeler. The latter was also involved with a Soviet Embassy official and there was public concern about a risk to national security. Profumo told Parliament that there was 'no impropriety whatsoever"[9] in his relationship with Keeler, but as details of the affair emerged (such as naked swimming at a party at Cliveden House) he resigned. When combined with other scandals of the time, such as the blackmailing of an Admiralty official, John Vassall, by the KGB, the Profumo affair undermined the government's reputation. In contrast, Labour, led by Harold Wilson from 1963, was able to put forward a modernising agenda using the term 'white heat of technology' to summarise its energy for change. At the 1964 election it looked far more able than a sleazy Conservative Party, by this time led by the tweedy aristocrat Alec Douglas-Home, to lead Britain in the 1960s, a decade which was already beginning to swing.

MEDIOCRE PRIME MINISTERS – HAROLD MACMILLAN

Harold Macmillan (1894–1986) served as Prime Minister from 1957 to 1963 and presided over a period of high economic growth in which he could rightly claim that Britain had 'never had it so good'. Macmillan can take little credit for the benign global economic conditions, and indeed he has been seriously criticised for failing to do anything about the threat of inflation, which he had identified as a problem. However, Macmillan was a significant figure on the international scene. He took over at a time when Britain's reputation was severely damaged after the debacle of the Suez crisis, which had forced out his predecessor, Eden. Macmillan successfully rebuilt Britain's relationship with the USA, especially through a close relationship with President John F. Kennedy who came to office in 1961. Meanwhile, Macmillan played a significant role in the peaceful ending of British rule in several African countries. Although Macmillan's government had become increasingly tarnished with sleaze by the time he resigned in 1963, it was ill health which forced him out of office. Ironically, he had been incorrectly diagnosed as having an inoperable cancer, but when it became clear that this was not the case, he had already stood down.

Despite such controversies, we can still see much consensus between parties at this time. Harold Macmillan's reaction to pressure within his party for a new direction illustrates resistance to moving away from the centre ground. As Prime Minister, Macmillan made much of his success in presiding over an economy that was growing. The phrase 'You've never had it so good' became closely associated with him after he used words to that effect at a Conservative rally in Bedford in July 1957. However, he had an inkling that the growth may not be

POOR PRIME MINISTERS

It may seem odd to describe Winston Churchill (1874–1965) as a poor Prime Minister. Yet in the context of post-1945 politics, that is just what he was. Old age and illness left him very frail during his time as PM in 1951–5 and he was a shadow of his wartime self when he had arguably been Britain's greatest ever PM. In the 1950s, Churchill was symptomatic of the crisis of leadership which faced the Conservative Party for much of the 1950s and 1960s. In some ways the party was struggling to find someone as great as the wartime Churchill and even the man himself could not fill that role post-war. When Churchill was succeeded by Anthony Eden (1897–1977), who had been the heir apparent for years, it looked like there might be new direction and vitality for the party. But Eden was gone within two years, ostensibly handing over to Macmillan on health grounds, but in reality damaged below the waterline by the Suez crisis (see Chapter 8). Because of Suez, Eden is quite often seen as Britain's worst post-war Prime Minister. The other claimant to that title is Alec Douglas-Home (1903–95) who was Prime Minister for barely a year in 1963–4. His time was limited by the fact that when he took over, a general election was imminent and he had little time to make his mark. The dominant image of him is as the 14th Earl of Home (a title he held before becoming Prime Minister), more at home on the grouse moor than in the Swinging London of the 1960s. Compared to Eden, though, he made few mistakes.

sustainable and that it was important to show restraint in how the proceeds of growth were spent. Other Conservatives shared these concerns, especially Peter Thorneycroft, then the Chancellor, who believed that steadily increasing public expenditure would lead to higher inflation. When in 1958 Macmillan decided that, despite his doubts, high spending should continue, Thorneycroft resigned. This row set the Conservatives firmly on maintaining the policies of consensus but it began to open up a fissure in the Conservative Party which would erupt in the 1970s.

Entirely outside party politics was the situation in Northern Ireland. From the mid-1960s there had been pressure within Northern Ireland for reforms to institutions and laws which were widely held to discriminate against the Catholic minority in the population. Reforms came slowly – too slow for some, but too quickly for others. By the summer of 1969 a state of virtual civil war existed in some of Northern Ireland's towns and cities. When British troops were deployed to keep order, although initially welcomed by Catholics who saw them as protectors, they soon became a target for the largest paramilitary group, the Irish Republican Army (or IRA), which wanted Northern Ireland to be part of a fully independent United Ireland. The brief honeymoon with the Catholic population ended within months and British troops came to be seen as a bulwark of the Protestant-dominated state. By 1972, the situation was so bad that Northern Ireland's devolved Parliament had been suspended, with rule from London in its place. However, in the late 1960s, nobody could have guessed that thirty years of 'The Troubles' lay ahead.

None of this divided the main parties in Britain. Much more problematic was the role of trades unions. By the late 1960s, successive strikes were making the leaders of all parties concerned that the unions held too much unaccountable power. Harold Wilson gave Barbara Castle, the Secretary of

State for Employment, the task of coming up with recommendations for constraining union power. Her proposals in a government white paper, *In Place of Strife* (1969), included a requirement for unions to ballot all members before going on strike and were vigorously opposed by union leaders. In the face of this, the government dropped its scheme and unions were to become the central problem of British politics in the 1970s.

MEDIOCRE PRIME MINISTERS – HAROLD WILSON

The tone of politics in the Swinging Sixties was set by Harold Wilson (1916–95) who was Prime Minister from 1964 to 1970 and then again from 1974 to 1976. Wilson made 'modernisation' an overt goal and used the rhetoric of the 'modern'. He saw technology as the driver of a better future and wanted a new meritocratic society forged in its 'white heat'. Under Wilson, there was a massive expansion of comprehensive education, in addition to a raft of legislation which created a more liberal society. This suited the mood of the times which, like Blair, Wilson was great at judging. Consequently, Wilson did much to break down the image of politics and politicians as stuffy and aristocratic. He was one of three Prime Ministers who rose from humble origins through grammar school to Oxford University (the other two being Thatcher and Heath) and Wilson seemed to embody the idea that everyone could be successful in post-war Britain. He astutely courted celebrities, securing the award of MBEs to the Beatles, and remarking that England only seem to win the football World Cup (in 1966) under a Labour government. It should also be said that Wilson was highly effective at navigating divides within the Labour Party, keeping it broadly united on such controversial issues as the Vietnam War and membership of the European Economic Community. None of this makes Wilson a great Prime Minister, but it made him the supreme political fixer of his day.

MOVERS AND SHAKERS – BARBARA CASTLE

In her time, Barbara Castle (1910–2002) was one of the most prominent figures in politics. Partly, Castle was known for the relative rarity of women ministers at the time. Had the Labour Party ever chosen a woman as leader in the 1960s or 1970s, it would most likely have been her. She first gained public prominence in the later 1940s and 1950s as someone who was willing to speak her mind, especially on international issues, and was part of the Bevanite left of the Labour Party. However, it was her career as a minister which gave her a prominent place in the public mind. As Minister of Transport in 1965–8, she introduced the breathalyser to try to tackle 'drunk driving'. In 1968–70 she was Secretary of State for Employment in which role she secured the landmark Equal Pay Act. This gave women the right to equal pay: it had previously been legal for employers to pay men more than women for the same work. In the same role, she was also embroiled in rows with unions through her *In Place of Strife* proposals. Although these failed, they put her in the public eye, as did her later introduction of the earnings link for pensions while Secretary of State for Social Services in 1974–6. Consequently, Barbara Castle was someone who became very prominent simply by doing what ministers do.

Legislators had more success in passing a series of liberalising measures in the mid to late 1960s, which arose from and contributed to the new air of freedom which marked the Swinging Sixties. A series of laws regarding matters of life, death and morality were brought in on a largely cross-party basis. Homosexuality (in private and between consenting adults over the age of twenty-one) was decriminalised in 1967, as was abortion. Capital punishment was suspended in 1965, while divorce on the basis of 'marital breakdown' was allowed from 1969.

1970–9: the Sick Man of Europe

Most commentators expected Harold Wilson to win again in the 1970 election and it was something of a surprise that Edward Heath led the Conservatives to victory instead. This is sometimes attributed to the publication of poor economic statistics just before the election, which made people concerned about Labour's stewardship of the economy. Heath had certainly been critical of Labour on the economy and public spending, and intended to behave differently in government. At a conference of the Conservative Shadow Cabinet at Selsdon Park prior to the election, Heath set out an agenda which involved reducing spending and getting tough on the unions. This was seen to be going back to an earlier form of Conservatism, and rejecting aspects of the post-war consensus, in the way that Thorneycroft had wanted back in 1958.

Heath certainly entered government with the intention of carrying out these policies. The Industrial Relations Act (1971) established a special court to enforce pay agreements made through collective bargaining. The 1971 budget reduced income tax and cut some areas of public spending. However, Heath did not manage to face down a miners' strike in 1972 (they got three times the pay increase they were originally offered) and dock workers also went on strike successfully in the same year. Meanwhile, inflation was rising and Britain was importing ever more manufactured goods than it was exporting. British industry simply did not seem to be competitive in global markets and, compared to most other European countries, Britain was in the doldrums, becoming widely known as the 'Sick Man of Europe'.

Heath's approach to these problems was heavily constrained by his generational attitudes. In part, he felt that joining the European Economic Community, which Britain did from 1 January 1973 (see Chapter 8), would help solve Britain's economic problems and, more widely, contribute towards peace in Europe. He was also willing to spend a great deal to bail out failing industries so that they would not have to lay off workers. So, for example, Rolls Royce was nationalised in 1971 rather than being allowed to go bankrupt. Moreover, the unions remained extremely powerful and the miners, buoyed up by their success in 1972, went on strike again in late 1973, at this stage only refusing to work overtime and weekends. By this time, the effects of the Arab–Israeli war were having a huge effect on fuel prices and the miners well knew that there was no cheap oil alternative to coal to keep the power stations going. By January 1974, electricity was becoming so scarce that businesses were forced to work a three-day week to save energy. In homes, the lights were liable to go out at any point due to regular power cuts. When the miners went on full strike in February 1974, Heath sought an election, telling the country that it had to choose between rule by Parliament or rule by the unions.

The country seemed to be unclear about its answer to this question, with Labour and the Conservatives almost neck and neck when the votes were counted. One reason for this close result was that at various times since the early 1960s, voters had shown an increasing willingness to opt for parties other than Labour and the Conservatives. That partly meant Plaid Cymru and the Scottish National Party in Wales and Scotland, but throughout Britain it meant the Liberal Party. The Liberals had shown that they could win by-elections with protest votes against the government from the late 1950s, and occasionally did well in opinion polls, but this had not translated into a significant showing at a general election until February 1974. In that election, they increased their seats from six to fourteen, but more importantly, their vote share went up from 7.5% to 19.3%.

Despite the lack of an overall majority, Harold Wilson, as incoming Labour Prime Minister, did not seek to form a coalition (although Heath did have unsuccessful talks with the Liberals to try to save his political skin). Instead, Wilson led a minority government before holding another election in October 1974 which gave him a narrow majority. One of Wilson's first acts was to repeal Heath's union legislation, which he did in return for the unions agreeing to restrain their wage demands voluntarily. That pledge did not last long and the story of the rest of the decade is one of Labour (led by James Callaghan after Wilson stood down in 1976) struggling to deal with an economy which was falling apart and unions which made ever more demands on the public purse.

The crunch came in the summer of 1976 when the Treasury was incapable of meeting the demands on it for spending. Callaghan went to the International Monetary Fund and secured a loan of nearly £4 billion, but this was only given in return for a pledge that public spending would be reduced by £3 billion annually. Since the interests of union members were the targets of many cuts, the unions were enraged. The government was steadily losing its majority through by-election losses and a brief pact with the Liberal Party (the 'Lib-Lab Pact') only held off the inevitable. By the winter of 1978, there were strikes throughout the public sector. A symbol of the nation's paralysis was that refuse collectors were on strike and piles of rubbish began to collect on the streets. In March 1979, in the wake of what became known as the 'Winter of Discontent', Callaghan lost a vote of confidence in Parliament. Inflation stood at over ten percent. Yet if the unions had been aggrieved about their treatment at the hands of a Labour government, they were about to face an even tougher opponent.

MOVERS AND SHAKERS – ENOCH POWELL

Enoch Powell (1912–98) presided over aspects of consensus politics quite happily, not least as Minister of Health in 1960–3. Yet Powell was outspoken on three issues which made him an extremely newsworthy figure. The first of these was levels of public spending. As far back as 1958, when he was Financial Secretary to the Treasury, he came to the view that Conservatives should be reducing state spending. He even resigned from office with Peter Thorneycroft in protest over Harold Macmillan's spending plans. This was a theme to which he returned in the early 1970s and although he had managed to marginalise himself from the mainstream Conservative Party by this time, he was the most prominent Conservative to take this line, well before, for example, Keith Joseph did so. That Powell was so marginalised from his party was because he had by 1968 become a vociferous opponent of immigration into the UK from former colonies. He said in an infamous speech that he foresaw 'rivers of blood' running in the streets if immigration was not checked. Although he was certainly not calling for violence, it was an inflammatory speech which led Heath to sack him from the Shadow Cabinet. Powell's formal separation from his party came in 1974 when he left the Conservatives over Europe. He did not support British membership of the EEC and called on people to vote against his party (which was then far more enthusiastic about Europe than Labour was) before he moved to become an Ulster Unionist MP. Throughout, Powell's influence came through speaking for many who did not see a party which represented their views. As such, he was a mover and shaker simply by being in the news and creating debate.

1979–97: Thatcherism

Nobody had expected Margaret Thatcher to be elected as leader of the Conservative Party when she challenged Heath in 1975. She was simply seen as a 'stalking horse', somebody who would run against the existing leader to see how much discontent there really was, prior to bigger beasts (in this case, people like William Whitelaw) entering a proper leadership race if Heath was damaged enough to stand down. But she did so well in the first ballot against Heath that she had the momentum to continue in the next round of the election and emerged as the surprise winner, the first woman to lead a British political party.

MOVERS AND SHAKERS – KEITH JOSEPH

Keith Joseph (1918–94) had a pretty unremarkable career as a Conservative minister in the 1960s and 1970s. When the Conservatives lost office in 1974, nobody would have predicted that Joseph would very rapidly become one of the most influential political thinkers of his party, let alone of the country, and that he would play a crucial role in shaping the next Conservative government. Yet he did that, and, unusually for a British politician, he did it on the basis of zealous pursuit of ideology. He left office in 1974 convinced that the Conservatives needed a radical change of direction. He soon subscribed to New Right thinking, inspired by Friedrich von Hayek, Joseph Schumpeter and Milton Friedman, which led Conservatives to the view that the size and role of the state needed to be cut back drastically. He pushed these ideas within the Conservative Party, especially using the Centre for Policy Studies, and was influential in persuading Margaret Thatcher that the party should adopt a 'small state' and promote entrepreneurism. When he became Secretary of State for Industry in 1979, he issued senior civil servants with a reading list illustrating this new ideological direction. Joseph was never one to court public opinion: as an ideologue he was never popular, and that limited his effectiveness in the persuasive role of a minister, but it is hard to deny his influence.

THATCHER SWEEPS TO POWER (MAY 1979)

	Seats	Votes (no.)	Votes (%)
Conservative	339	13,697,690	43.9
Labour	269	11,532,218	36.9
Liberal	11	4,313,804	13.8
Northern Ireland parties	12	695,889	2.2
Scottish National Party	2	504,259	1.6
Plaid Cymru	2	132,544	0.4
Others	0	343,674	1.2

Turnout: 76.0%

Other than a sense of offering homespun wisdom about the need to balance budgets ('as any housewife knows', as she said), it was not quite clear where Thatcher would take her party in policy terms. However, there were plenty of ideas on the New Right about where to go. Aside from Peter Thorneycroft, Enoch Powell had been a prominent Conservative opponent of high spending for many years, although he had marginalised himself from the rest of the party due to the anti-immigration stance he took from 1968.

By the time Thatcher became leader, Powell was an Ulster Unionist MP, not a Conservative. The role of tribune of the New Right therefore fell to Keith Joseph. Under his influence, ideas of a small state carrying out minimal public expenditure became the Conservative fashion in the late 1970s and provided the party with the intellectual confidence to dismantle the thinking of the post-war consensus. This message proved appealing to the voters in the 1979 general election.

In the first term, the economy suffered a scaling back which many commentators saw as akin to slash and burn. Unemployment topped three million, and was most marked in areas where manufacturing had once been the main employer, as the government simply refused to continue the practice of giving vast state funding to industry. Conservative ministers said that government should no longer be in the business of picking winners and backing losers through state aid. Beginning with British Aerospace, the British Sugar Corporation, and Cable and Wireless in 1981, Thatcher's governments sold off massive chunks of nationalised industry. By 1990, such major industries as British Petroleum, British Steel, Rover and Jaguar had gone back into the private sector. So too had the utilities: gas, water and electricity. Meanwhile, Thatcher tried to reduce public spending in other ways. For example, in 1981, benefit payments were linked to prices rather than earnings, which meant that they rose more slowly. However, although cuts were perceived to be taking place in core aspects of public services, this was actually a simplistic impression. In the NHS, spending rose in real terms through the 1980s, although not by enough to match the expectations which people had of their health service.

In tandem with trying to reduce public spending, the Conservatives aimed to reduce the overall level of tax which was paid. The headline figures of income tax rates gave the impression that they did this, with their first budget cutting the basic rate of income tax from thirty-three percent to thirty percent and the top rate from eighty-three percent to sixty percent. Later cuts brought the basic rate down to twenty-five percent by 1988 and the top rate down to forty percent. However, value added tax (VAT), which hits the poor hardest because it takes no account of ability to pay, was increased from eight percent to fifteen percent in 1979. Overall, the proportion of the nation's wealth taken in tax actually rose by just over one percent between 1979 and 1990, so in their aim to reduce the size of the state, the Conservatives under Thatcher failed. What the Conservatives did do, however, was reduce the amount of redistribution between rich and poor because of the impact of VAT. Since Thatcher wanted to reward those who generated profits, they would have seen that as a success.

They were more successful in achieving other goals. The powers of the unions were dramatically reduced. Three Employment Acts (1980, 1982 and 1988) and the Trade Unions Act (1984) steadily constrained union powers far beyond the proposals put forward by Labour in the late 1960s, which were resisted by trades unionists. The union movement's authority suffered greatly from the defeat of the miners in their year-long strike of 1984–5. Under the terms of the 1984 act, unions had to hold secret ballots before any strike action, while secondary strikes (those in support of a dispute at another employer) were outlawed in 1982. Related to the limitation of union powers, the Conservatives were able to claim plausibly that they had brought about an economic miracle in Britain. After its 1985 peak of three million, unemployment fell steadily, and by 1986, inflation was at 2.5%, having been at twenty-one percent in 1980. Privatisation and the expansion of shared ownership were popular. Overall, the British economy seemed to be growing at a far better rate than many overseas competitors. The Conservatives claimed to have cured the 'British disease' of uncompetitiveness, restoring entrepreneurialism to the economy.

GREAT PRIME MINISTERS – MARGARET THATCHER

Margaret Thatcher (1925–2013) will always be significant in politics for being the first and currently only woman to have been Prime Minister. Indeed, except for (in 1994) Margaret Beckett's and (in 2010 and 2015) Harriet Harman's brief tenures as acting Labour

GREAT PRIME MINISTERS –
MARGARET THATCHER (*cont.*)

leaders, she remains the only woman have led either of the two main political parties. However, it is her approach to policy and her leadership style which are her lasting impact on politics.

To some extent her views were informed by basic instincts about the role of government and the need for fiscal frugality, but they were also part of a New Right neo-liberal consensus which influenced politicians in other countries, most notably President Ronald Reagan in the USA. This led to a major shift in a number of areas of policy which unpicked the Attlee consensus. Thatcher achieved these changes against a significant (possibly majority) body of opinion in her Cabinet which was against them.

The ability to do that rested on her style. During the 1970s, politicians had flipped and flopped in the face of negative public opinion. One would imagine that the public likes to be listened to, but when Thatcher said, 'You turn if you want to. The lady's not for turning,'[10] she made a virtue of not doing so and was popular because of it. People did not generally 'like' Thatcher, but they trusted her and saw her as a strong leader. Consequently, she won three sizeable election majorities and set a new political agenda more than any politician since Attlee.

In public services, Thatcher also led reforms. Her flagship policy was the Housing Act (1980) which gave council tenants the right to buy their homes. Over one million were bought by 1988. This represented a scaling back of the size of council spending, a policy also pursued by the Conservatives in a series of local government reforms. These included the 1984 Rates Act, which gave central government the power to cap local rates at a certain level, due to concerns over high-spending 'Loony Left' councils. In the NHS, while Thatcher pledged that the basic principle of a free-to-use tax-funded system was safe in Conservative hands, she introduced an internal market (see Chapter 6) to try to boost efficiency. In education, a National Curriculum introduced greater central control over what was taught in schools, while parents were given more choice over which school their child went to (see Chapter 6).

In all of these reforms, the sense that Thatcher might be tough, but was telling it how it needed to be told, was incredibly effective in persuading the country that change was needed. For most of her eleven years in office she was seen as a strong and effective leader. That is not to say that she did not divide the country; far from it. The 1980s witnessed some of the most bitter social divisions that the country has ever seen, not only over economic problems. There were riots in many of Britain's inner cities in the summer of 1981, partly related to tensions between members of ethnic minorities and the police. However, Thatcher consistently managed to persuade 42–43% of the electorate that she was the strong leader Britain needed, not only on the basis of domestic policy but also for her tough stance on foreign affairs. Her leadership during, for example, the Falklands War, is discussed in detail later on (see Chapter 8).

It should also be said that Thatcher was aided by the opposition parties being weak throughout the 1980s. Labour split in 1981, with a group of prominent centrist Labour politicians forming the Social Democratic Party and then fighting elections jointly with the Liberal Party as the SDP–Liberal Alliance. But that was itself troubled by having two leaders (one for each party in the Alliance), while the remaining Labour Party fought the 1983 election on the most left-wing manifesto ever put to the British electorate. It did not suit the mood of the times and was dubbed by a former Labour minister, Gerald Kaufman, as 'the longest suicide note in history'.[11]

MOVERS AND SHAKERS – THE 'GANG OF FOUR'

The 'Gang of Four' is the name given to those who formed the Social Democratic Party in 1981: Roy Jenkins (1920–2003), David Owen (1938–), Bill Rodgers (1928–) and Shirley Williams (1930–). They had all held office as Labour ministers, with Jenkins serving as both Home Secretary and Chancellor of the Exchequer, and Owen as Foreign Secretary, but it was their formation of the SDP that made them shapers of British politics. They decided that the Labour Party had become too extreme to offer a social democratic alternative to the Conservatives and that a new party was necessary. That move had very profound consequences. It divided the opposition to Thatcher and was one factor which allowed her to win in 1983 and 1987. It offered a new political force through the Alliance with the Liberal Party, which eventually led to the formation of the Liberal Democrats. The SDP's formation also briefly moved the Labour Party to the left, before a new generation tried to move it back to the centre. In all of these developments, the actions of the Gang of Four were crucial factors.

Thatcher appeared to have led Britain to greatness again, and to be the only viable Prime Minister. Yet by 1990, her leadership was showing cracks. The Community Charge (commonly known as the Poll Tax) was to replace local rates with a charge levied on all individuals regardless of ability to pay. Public anger over the Poll Tax was so great that major protests were mounted. Some of these resulted in riots, the most notable being one in Trafalgar Square. Meanwhile, there were tensions within the Conservative Party over what many senior figures saw as Thatcher's overly negative approach to Europe. The Labour Party had begun to look more like an alternative government under Neil Kinnock. Consequently, the Conservatives started to lose by-elections both to Labour and to the Liberal Democrats, formed in 1988 when the

Liberals and SDP merged. In the face of such results, and poor opinion polls, Thatcher was challenged for the leadership by Michael Heseltine. Thatcher was badly damaged by the challenge and stood down.

MICHAEL HESELTINE

A significant influence was exerted on the Conservative Party and politics in the 1980s and 1990s by Michael Heseltine (1933–). Heseltine, nicknamed 'Tarzan' for waving the Parliamentary mace at Labour MPs after a vote on nationalisation, was one of the great platform speakers of the Conservative Party in the 1970s and 1980s. As such, he became an obvious candidate for ministerial office when the party gained power in 1979, and was also seen as a future leader. Consequently, he became one of those pivotal figures to whom the public and journalists listened, simply because they thought he was senior in his party. Much public attention focused on the extent to which he might offer a different type of leadership to Thatcher, and there was some sense, perhaps exaggerated, that he was on the more 'wet' wing of the party than Thatcher's closest allies. 'Wets' were opposed to the tone of politics pursued by Thatcher and wanted a return to more consensual policies. When he resigned from office in 1986 during a dispute about the future of Westland Helicopters, at the core of the debate was the question of whether Britain should be closer to Europe than America in the organisation of defence procurement. That was a proxy debate for the one that would soon divide the party over Britain's wider role in Europe. From outside government, Heseltine became the most obvious leader-in-waiting until he challenged Thatcher in 1990, ultimately causing her resignation from office. Having wielded the knife, the party was reluctant to allow him to wear the crown and he never achieved his ambition of the top job in British politics. However, Heseltine remains a clear example of those who maintain a high public profile through sheer force of personality.

The Conservatives chose John Major as their leader, who simply continued Thatcher's policies in many areas. In particular, he went further than her on privatisation, with the railways being sold off. But there were also symbolic changes, such as the ditching of the Poll Tax. Moreover, Major offered a far less confrontational approach to politics, even if it was, in the words of Kenneth Clarke, 'Thatcherism with a human face'.[12] Major's leadership did enough to persuade the country that it had got the change of government it wanted. So in the 1992 general election, partly on the basis of Major's personal style, the Conservatives squeaked home to a narrow victory when it had looked like Labour would win. Yet after this victory, Major was unable to keep the lid on an impassioned debate in his party over Europe which made his leadership look weak. In 1995, he stood down and faced a leadership election in an effort to make his critics 'put up or shut up'. In the short term it worked, but ultimately it merely reinforced the image that his party was divided and unleadable.

To make matters worse, soon after electoral victory in 1992, the economic miracle the Conservatives claimed to have conjured went badly wrong. In September 1992 a run on the pound caused Britain to leave the European exchange rate mechanism and a series of economic problems afflicted the country. At no point between 1993 and 1997 did it look like the Conservatives could win a general election and Major delayed calling one for as long as was legally possible. Meanwhile, a host of Conservative MPs were the subject of scandals which turned many voters off a party which seemed to be mired in sleaze. When the election came, the Conservatives suffered a devastating defeat as Labour swept to victory, helped by the rise of 'tactical voting' which saw anti-Conservative voters back whichever of Labour or the Liberal Democrats had the best chance of beating the Conservatives in each seat.

LABOUR'S GREATEST ELECTION VICTORY (MAY 1997)

	Seats	Votes (no.)	Votes (%)
Conservative	165	9,600,940	30.7
Labour	418	13,517,911	43.2
Liberal Democrats	46	5,243,440	16.8
Northern Ireland parties	18	790,778	2.5
Scottish National Party	6	622,260	1.9
Plaid Cymru	4	161,030	0.5
Others	1	1,361,701	4.4
Turnout: 71.5%			

1997–2010: a new consensus?

Strictly speaking it was not Labour but 'New' Labour which won the party's greatest ever victory. Labour had begun to reform itself following the 1983 election defeat. It became, essentially, less left-wing, dropping policies such as withdrawal from Europe and NATO, unilateral nuclear disarmament and nationalisation. It also reformed its own party structures so that the trades unions had less power. Meanwhile, a slick communications strategy was developed under the leadership of Neil Kinnock, pioneered by Labour's communications director, Peter Mandelson.

When Labour lost again in 1987, it looked afresh at why it had done so. One conclusion it reached was that it needed a leader who was seen as a credible Prime Minister. Brilliant as an orator though he was, Kinnock was often portrayed in the media as being intellectually lightweight. Labour also concluded that it needed to be seen as credible on the economy and that it still had work to do to shed its image as a

EFFECTIVE PARTY LEADERS – NEIL KINNOCK

After two heavy election defeats in 1979 and 1983, Labour turned to Neil Kinnock (1942–) to change its electoral fortunes. Kinnock was not an obvious moderniser, coming as he did from a mining community in South Wales and the party's 'soft left'. Yet these credentials made him the ideal person to drag Labour away from the hard-left manifesto on which it had stood in 1983. Kinnock was clear that the party must stand up for the poor and pursue policies that would help them. However, he believed just as strongly that the Labour Party was letting these people down if it failed to get elected. Without a Labour government, his argument ran, there would be a Conservative government, and that would do nothing to help the poor. A wide range of policy changes ensued, but Kinnock's reforms were also about the way the Labour Party conducted itself. He reduced the powers of the unions within the party, and introduced a more professional approach to party communications. In his day, Kinnock was a brilliant orator, but he was prone to giving confused and confusing answers to policy questions. His personal appearance was mocked by the press and in contrast to Thatcher he was not seen as a strong leader. Yet he laid the foundations for New Labour, and the victory in 1997 was to some extent Kinnock's success just as it was Blair's.

high-tax party. The solid and responsible John Smith ticked both boxes (even though he had been their Shadow Chancellor in 1992 and had developed the tax plans that backfired at that election) and he was in an ideal position to make Labour seem a credible alternative government when the economy started to go wrong. His sudden death from a heart attack in 1994 shocked everyone. Labour was consistently ahead in the polls at that time and Smith had looked like the Prime Minister in waiting.

To fill Smith's shoes, the party turned to Tony Blair, who was very different to Smith both in character and background, but had a certain star quality about him. As Shadow Home Secretary he had tried to shed Labour's image of being a party that was soft on crime. In 1993, he said that the party should be 'tough on crime and tough on the underlying causes of crime'.[13] This reforming approach to policy continued when he was elected as leader following Smith's death. Blair was determined to appeal to middle England and one of his reforms symbolised that goal above all others. He persuaded the Labour Party to drop Clause IV of its constitution, which committed the party to nationalisation. Instead, words relating to 'common endeavour' and spreading opportunity to 'the many, not the few' were inserted. More than anything else, this change told the public that Labour had dropped its old approach to the economy and was now part of mainstream British politics. Some critics saw this as simply embracing the central tenets of neo-liberalism which had informed Thatcherism. Certainly, Labour was now proposing no major change to the fundamentals of the economic system that had developed in the 1980s, not even any changes to trades union legislation. Blair could justifiably describe his party as 'New' Labour and this label, though never formally adopted as the party's name, soon appeared in all Labour publicity.

Labour's success in 1997 can also be attributed to its focus on issues which were of major concern to the electorate. Moreover, in its 'Five Pledges' announced in 1996, it focused on relatively limited goals by which it asked to be judged. In some ways the most significant pledge was one to do nothing: 'No rise in income tax rates'. Making such a pledge was unheard of in Labour history and it told the electorate that Tony Blair and Gordon Brown (the Chancellor in waiting) were serious about New Labour being New.

EFFECTIVE PARTY LEADERS – PADDY ASHDOWN

Leaders of third parties have a difficult time. They have to make their party appear relevant in debates in which it is far too easy for the media to focus on only two parties. In their different ways, at different times, but only briefly, various leaders of the Liberals, SDP and Liberal Democrats have done this. However, the leader who did this in the most sustained manner was Jeremy John Durham 'Paddy' Ashdown (1941–). He took over the Liberal Democrats in 1988 soon after the Liberals and SDP merged. The party was not even agreed on what to call itself and at one point in the early days of his leadership it stood at three percent in the opinion polls. As he himself would point out later, as polls have a margin of error of plus or minus three percent, it is conceivable that such a result actually meant that the party had no support whatsoever. With dogged determination, Ashdown travelled around the country convincing party activists that it really was worth carrying on, and he began to persuade voters that the Liberal Democrats had something to offer. In the early 1990s, he also acquired a reputation as an expert on the Balkans, which made him a respected figure in his own right, while at the same time positioning his party as one which could help remove the Conservatives from office. Although the coalition with Blair which he wanted never came to fruition, his party doubled its parliamentary representation in 1997, laying the foundations for later leaders to make further progress. In the early days of Ashdown's leadership, two-party politics looked like reasserting itself. By the end, three-party politics was more real than at any time since the 1920s.

Middle England had nothing to be worried about in these pledges. Indeed, after extensive polling and consultation with focus groups, Labour knew that speaking about class sizes, crime, the NHS and jobs was just what the floating voter wanted to hear.

LABOUR'S 'FIVE PLEDGES' IN 1997

- Cut class sizes to thirty or under for five-, six- and seven-year-olds by using money from the assisted places scheme.
- Fast-track punishment for young offenders by halving the time from arrest to sentencing.
- Cut NHS waiting lists by treating an extra 100,000 patients as a first step, by releasing £100 million saved from NHS red tape.
- Get 250,000 under-twenty-five-year-olds off benefits and into work by using money from a windfall levy on privatised utilities.
- No rise in income tax rates, cut VAT on heating to five percent, and inflation and interest rates as low as possible.

By 2002, Labour had met its five pledges and been radical in a range of areas, often more radical than it cared to say so as not to frighten the voters. Arguably the most dramatic changes came in the realm of constitutional affairs. There was devolution to Scotland, Wales and Northern Ireland. In the latter case, Tony Blair's role as peacemaker brought him worldwide plaudits. Further constitutional reforms saw the introduction of Freedom of Information legislation, independence of the Bank of England (which was a policy that had been in the Liberal Democrat manifesto in 1997 but not the Labour one) and proportional representation used for elections to the European Parliament. This agenda was implemented with the support of the Liberal Democrats, who had agreed a programme with Labour prior to the election and sat on a Joint Cabinet Committee with Labour ministers from 1997 in order to implement the policies. This was a highly unusual move: no member of an opposition party had sat on a Cabinet committee since the 1930s (when disarmament was being discussed).

Labour was also bold in its increases in public spending. Although it stuck to Conservative spending plans for its first two years in office, growth in the economy was such that tax yields were rising. Labour could thus spend more without having to increase tax rates. In health, Labour pledged to reach the European average of spending around eight percent of gross domestic product on health by 2004 and it met that target. By 2009, spending on the NHS had increased by at least fifty percent in real terms when compared to 1997. In schools, spending per pupil was set to rise from £2,500 in 1997 to £6,600 in 2010.

Yet New Labour was also seen as being timid in government. Pro-Europeans said it missed an opportunity to join the Euro (although many praise it for that), and many saw it as having been too slow to invest in public services. Students and their families have been vehemently against the introduction of university tuition fees (which Labour initially pledged not to do), believing that Labour should have fought harder for free education. The persistence of poverty was criticised by many commentators: even though policies such as the Working Families Tax Credit undoubtedly helped many, there was little effort by Labour to make the rigorous case for redistribution, which many expected from a Labour government. That was despite the fact that, from 1997 to 2010, the incomes of the poorest ten percent of households rose by thirteen percent, while the incomes of the richest ten percent fell by almost nine percent. The Institute for Fiscal Studies attributes that to the tax and benefits system.[14]

Despite this timidity, or perhaps because of it, Tony Blair led Labour to three election victories. Yet the seeds of Labour's subsequent deep unpopularity had already been planted before Labour won the 2005 election. Britain's involvement in the war in Iraq from 2003 (see Chapter 8) made Tony Blair so unpopular that he pledged not to serve a full term if he won the election. That helped to reassure people that Blair would

GREAT PRIME MINISTERS – TONY BLAIR

Most political commentators and academics have no doubt that Attlee and Thatcher deserve to be called 'great' Prime Ministers. Tony Blair (1953–) has some claim to be added to the list. This is not so much due to policy. Undoubtedly, Blair led from the front on a number of issues, especially the war in Iraq, though his role remains a controversial legacy. Moreover, the levels of investment which flooded into public services during his time in office did much to tackle the severe deprivation which many schools and hospitals faced under the Conservatives. However, in many areas of policy all that Blair did was preside over the system he inherited from the Conservatives, with creeping marketisation of public services, a neo-liberal approach to the economy and taxation, and no changes to trades union legislation even where Labour had opposed it vigorously in opposition.

Rather than policy, Blair's claim to greatness rests on being the only Labour leader to win three general elections, each with sizeable majorities. He did so on the basis of an instinctive understanding of the fears and foibles of the floating voters who determine elections. Despite the fact that he was seen from an early stage as being a smooth salesman, people seemed not to mind. He spoke to their concerns and appeared to understand both Mondeo Man and Worcester Woman (media phrases for swing voters). When Labour took a decision to remove him, they did so because they thought he was electorally damaged and that they would fare better under Gordon Brown, which was actually what the opinion polls showed. However, polls are fickle and we may never see another Labour leader with Blair's unique and long-standing ability to connect with the public.

not try to continue in office for more than five years, and many believed that Gordon Brown would revive Labour's popularity – partly because opinion polls had been showing him to be more popular than Blair. For a few months it worked. Brown was doing so well that there was talk of an election being called in autumn 2007. But when Brown dithered, and eventually did not call an election, many media commentators and his opponents questioned his judgement.

Brown must have wished that he had gone to the country in 2007. Over 2008–9 the government suffered from two problems over which it had little control. First of all, the global recession made a major impact on Britain, particularly because the UK is so dependent on financial services as a driver of the economy and this sector was among the worst hit. Meanwhile, the government suffered more than the other parties over the *Daily Telegraph*'s investigation into MPs' expenses. Although it affected all parties, Labour seems to have taken more blame as the incumbent party and because the public felt that Brown had not acted as decisively as other party leaders. Brown was also damaged by the fact that prior to the credit crunch he had applauded the City of London's contribution to the British economy and claimed that he had put an end to the economic cycle of 'boom and bust'. Both positions haunted him as the economy collapsed. This is something of a tragedy for Brown personally. If there is any credit to be given to anybody for New Labour and its record in government, then Brown was as much the architect as Blair. By the end of his term of office, he could do little right: if he had found a way of turning base metals into gold, one expects he would have gained little credit from a public that was just fed up with Labour.

Brown's difficulties came at a time when there was a growing sense of British politics being in crisis. This was not something that suddenly happened in 2010. Turnouts in elections reached a post-war high of eighty-four percent in 1950, and were then usually around seventy-five percent until 1997. That election, despite all the enthusiasm that there was for a change in government, saw a post-war low of 71.5%, but in 2001 and 2005 there was a marked fall: 59.4%

and 61.2%. In 2010 the turnout rose a little to 65.1%. Such relative lack of interest in elections can partly be attributed to the public deciding that it does not matter which party is in power. There is also a sense that politics generally has far less influence on daily lives than it did from the 1950s to 1970s when government was responsible for running swathes of the economy through nationalised industries. Accompanying this has been a marked decline in what political scientists call 'partisan alignment': close identification of voters with parties along ideological and/or class lines. Put simply, people no longer think 'I am Labour' in the way that they did when many of the people in a street worked in the same factory, joined the same union and drank at the working men's club. To add to these general changes were some more specific factors in the 2000s. In 2001, the result was a foregone conclusion, so why bother voting? In 2005, many Labour voters stayed at home rather than back a Prime Minister who had gone to war too often for their liking, and there was no desire for a change to the Conservatives. In 2010, MPs' expenses tarred all politicians with the same brush. In such a situation, the incumbent always suffers, however much real responsibility they carry.

Even before the expenses issue came onto the agenda, opinion polls were consistently showing that a Conservative government led by David Cameron was likely to be the result of the next election. He managed to persuade the electorate that he had changed his party so that it had shed much of what made the voters reject it in 1997. After thirteen years of one party in power, the electorate simply seemed to want a change. While the Conservatives had been deeply unpopular for much of New Labour's time in government, many voters came to see the party as having changed under David Cameron, so they were both more repelled by Labour and more attracted to the Conservatives.

EFFECTIVE PARTY LEADERS – MICHAEL HOWARD

Just like Neil Kinnock, Michael Howard (1941–) laid the foundations for making his party electable when it was on the edge of oblivion. In 1997, it would have surprised many that six years later, Howard would become Conservative leader. He had been an unpopular Home Secretary in the last four years of Major's term of office and when he ran for the post of leader after Major stepped down, he came last of five candidates. Anne Widdecombe seemed to have forever tarnished his image when she said that there was 'something of the night'[15] about him.

Yet it remained the case that Howard was an effective parliamentary performer. That came to the fore when Iain Duncan Smith was Conservative leader. Duncan Smith was one of the all-time worst performers in Conservative history, unable to give a persuasive party conference speech and terrible at Prime Minister's Questions. Duncan Smith's best decision was to make Howard Shadow Chancellor, in which role he began to land punches on Gordon Brown and to articulate a clear Conservative view of what was wrong with Labour. Incredibly, his standing was such that when Duncan Smith resigned, Howard was elected unopposed as Conservative leader. In the 2005 election his party began to make inroads into the Labour majority and although the content of Conservative messages was criticised by opponents, that is always the case, and what Howard did was remind people what a Conservative message actually looked like. There had been a Conservative view, best articulated by Theresa May, that what made the Conservatives lose in 1997 was that they were seen as the 'nasty party'. Arguably, however, they suffered just as much from looking incompetent. It was not until Michael Howard came along in 2003 that that started to change. He laid the foundations which enabled them to get back into government in 2010.

THE END OF NEW LABOUR (2010)

	Seats	Votes (no.)	Votes (%)
Conservative	307	10,726,814	36.1
Labour	258	8,609,527	29.0
Liberal Democrats	57	6,836,824	23.0
Northern Ireland parties	18	622,551[1]	2.0
Scottish National Party	6	491,386	1.7
Plaid Cymru	3	165,394	0.6
Green	1	285,616	1.0
Others	1[2]	1,953,668	6.6
Turnout: 65.1%			

Notes

[1] Includes main Northern Ireland parties only: Democratic Unionist Party, Sinn Féin, Social Democratic and Labour Party, Alliance, Ulster Conservatives and Unionists, and Traditional Unionist Voice. Other parties, including Greens, are included in figures elsewhere in table.

[2] The one 'Other' MP is Sylvia Hermon in North Down, formerly an Ulster Unionist. Nearly half of the votes for 'Others' were for the UK Independence Party.

2010–15: Coalition and Austerity

Despite all the changes which David Cameron made to the Conservative Party the voters were still not inspired when it came to the election in May 2010. Back in 1997, there had been a strong sense that the public were desperate for the Conservatives to go, and were inspired by Labour enough to be enthusiastic about the alternative. In 2010, the mood was rather different and that was partly to do with Nick Clegg, the Liberal Democrat leader. Clegg entered the campaign unknown to the vast bulk of the population. The *Evening Standard* quoted one of Clegg's neighbours in Putney saying of him, before the election: 'He used to go into the local shop with shades on, but no one knew who he was, so he stopped wearing them.'[16] That all changed when, for the first time, the then three main party leaders took part in televised debates together. Previously, sitting Prime Ministers had resisted doing this, and there had been some hostility to the idea of allowing the third party to take part even if debates did happen. In the first debate of the campaign, Clegg emerged as the star with opinion polls showing a strong public consensus that he had won it. A few days after the first debate, one poll showed, according to the *Sunday Times*, 'Clegg nearly as popular as Churchill'. What was dubbed 'Cleggmania' had a huge impact on voting intentions. For much of the campaign, the Liberal Democrats seemed to be in second place behind the Conservatives, with a few polls even giving Clegg's party a narrow lead.[17] Clegg did not storm ahead in the second and third leaders' debates but he did hold his own in both and cemented his place as a serious contender.

Yet when it came to polling day, the Liberal Democrats barely improved on their 2005 vote share and actually lost seats. The twenty-three percent of the vote won by the party was even several points below what most opinion polls were showing only a day before voting took place. It was later widely held that close scrutiny of some Liberal Democrat policies on immigration and nuclear weapons had put off some voters. The party also suffered at the hands of tactical voters – people choosing to vote Labour or Conservative in order to keep the other party out.

Cameron did not win outright, but his position as leader of the largest party in a 'hung parliament' meant that Nick Clegg chose to negotiate first with him. It soon emerged that there were parallel negotiations with Labour but there were two problems with those. First, many Labour MPs did not want to make a deal with the Liberal Democrats. Second, Labour and the Liberal Democrats combined did not have a majority and would have relied on the support of other, smaller parties such as the SNP on key votes.

NEW POLITICS, NEW POLITICIANS?

When David Cameron (1966–) and Nick Clegg (1967–) became Prime Minister and Deputy Prime Minister in May 2010 the simple act of forming a coalition broke the mould of politics. Previously, there had been deals between parties in times of national crisis, but there had only been a hung parliament once since 1945 and even that had not led to a coalition. Perhaps even more surprising was the fact that the deal was done between the Conservatives and the Liberal Democrats. Especially since the early 1990s there has been much talk of a 'progressive' realignment in politics which would involve some form of collaboration between Labour and the Liberal Democrats, but there has been nothing similar about the Liberal Democrats and Conservatives. The other mould-breaker was a generational change. Cameron and Clegg come from a generation which first became aware of politics in the Thatcher years, rather than the years of social democratic consensus, and they do not remember a time when Britain was not part of Europe.

The collaboration was not all mould-breaking. Both Clegg and Cameron have spent much of their working lives in politics-related fields, continuing a trend of people entering Parliament in their thirties, without having pursued a career outside politics for any significant time. Meanwhile, they both come from very wealthy backgrounds. Between 1964 and 2010 there was only one privately educated Prime Minister (Tony Blair), but both Cameron and Clegg attended elite public schools and their Cabinet consisted of a high proportion of people from a similar background. The *Morning Star*'s front-page headline on the day after they took office said, 'Posh chaps take power'.[18]

What surprised many was how easy it appears to have been for two quite different parties to make concessions to each other. Of course, there was already agreement on some issues, such as the 'pupil premium' through which extra money would be targeted to schools with the most disadvantaged pupils. There was also a shared agenda on civil liberties. The Liberal Democrats gave up their policies on Trident and immigration, while both parties made concessions on Europe. The Conservatives accepted a number of Liberal Democrat policies on the environment and, crucially, agreed that there should be a referendum on electoral reform (which was held in 2011 and decisively rejected the idea of such reform). The existence of such an agreement on policy clearly represented a 'new' politics. It was quite unheard of. Almost as new was the formation of a full coalition Cabinet, the first peacetime one since the 1930s, with Nick Clegg as Deputy Prime Minister and four other Liberal Democrats joining him in the Cabinet. Liberal Democrat junior ministers also took up office throughout other government departments. That it had all been delivered through a first-past-the-post electoral system, after an election in which the two parties had been at each other's throats, made it all the more remarkable.

In government, there were immediate strains for the Liberal Democrats. Though a special conference of the party overwhelmingly backed the leadership's decision to form a coalition, those who had voted for the party were less enthusiastic. By 2011, support for the party in opinion polls was around ten percent, less than half of its 2010 vote share. Liberal Democrats took some solace in the fact that in the past few decades the party had traditionally scored lower in opinion polls than actual elections but the support never recovered, with polls in 2015 in the end matching the party's electoral support.[19] Liberal Democrat strategists hoped that by being in government, and by moderating the Conservatives, the party would in future attract 'centre' voters instead of those broadly on the centre-left or left who had swelled party support since the late 1990s.

This did not happen. In part, that was because of the issue of university tuition fees. The policy of scrapping fees had been a leading campaign issue for the party in 2010, making it especially appealing to those bothered about such fees. Meanwhile, Liberal Democrat candidates had signed a pledge, organised by the National

Union of Students, not to support any increase in fees if elected. When, in late 2010, it was announced that annual fees would be raised by the government from £3,000 to £9,000, the Liberal Democrats were tarnished by going against both their pledges to scrap fees and not to increase them. In fact, the party had been split, with twenty-one MPs voting against the increase, including former party leaders Charles Kennedy and Menzies Campbell, and eight abstaining. But it was the actions of the twenty-seven who voted in favour, including all the party's ministers, which suggested to people that Liberal Democrats could not be trusted in government. For a party which had made an election broadcast in 2010 about not breaking promises, this was especially difficult.[20]

Tuition fees were the high-profile issue which lost support for the Liberal Democrats, but it was concern about the economy which underpinned voters' unease about how the party was behaving in government, and this issue was the dominant one for all parties during of the coalition period. Going into the 2010 election, the three largest parties had all recognised that how to respond to the global recession which had been biting since 2008 was the crucial issue for the next government. Gordon Brown's government had held off some of the recession's worst effects by bailing out banks which were in danger of collapse. However, through doing so, and also due to a decline in tax revenues, the government was running a much larger deficit in public spending than it had done prior to the recession. Labour, the Conservatives and the Liberal Democrats all proposed some cuts in annual expenditure to reduce the deficit. However, Labour and the Liberal Democrats planned to do this at a slower rate than the Conservatives. As it happened, the coalition broadly pursued the Conservative plan in terms of the scale and timing of cuts. Moreover, the Conservatives persuaded the country that the deficit had been caused by Labour overspending throughout the 1997–2010 period, rather than by the global economic collapse. This created an atmosphere in which the centre ground of politics shifted to Conservative territory. Labour under Ed Miliband found it hard to shake off the tag of having been responsible for the country's economic problems, and the dominant idea in political debate was that there was little alternative to what became known as 'austerity'.

The success of the coalition's economic policy has been much debated. In the first place, it delivered cuts in public spending in the way that it wished to. Meanwhile, employment levels were sustained so there were not the high levels of unemployment seen in previous recessions. However, growth levels were significantly lower throughout 2010–15 than the government predicted. Some of that was down to the effects of problems in the Eurozone, but it also undermined the government's claim to be rebalancing the economy with a shift away from public spending towards a more dynamic private sector. This failure to deliver growth at the levels expected of course affected deficit reduction, which depended on tax revenues from a growing economy.[21] In March 2015, the verdict of the *Financial Times* was:

> The chancellor says he has halved the deficit as a share of national income. That is true, but the record is far less impressive than he planned in 2010, so deficit reduction must be regarded as a failure.
>
> The failure, however, came about because of excessive optimism about the strength of the UK economy, rather than the chancellor's spending cuts and tax increases. There is little evidence that it failed because of Mr Osborne's plans for the public finances.[22]

The other great issue of 2010–15 with long-term significance for the future of the UK was the possibility that Scotland might vote for independence. During 2012–13, in the light of the growing strength of the SNP (which had formed the government of Scotland since 2007), the Westminster and Scottish governments negotiated the terms of a referendum to be held on 18 September 2014 on the question 'Should Scotland be an independent country?' A long campaign ensued. There were times when it looked as if the independence campaign had a real chance of success and many unionists feared that the 'Yes' vote might actually win.[23] On a remarkably high turnout of 84.59%, 'No' was the favoured answer with 55.3% against 44.7% for 'Yes'. However, support for independence had grown during the campaign, reinvigorating Scottish politics.

The issue has not gone away. In his reaction to the referendum vote, David Cameron raised the idea of 'English votes for English laws', which seemed to some to undermine his pledge that there would be further devolution to Scotland (even though he also announced a plan to consider such proposals).[24] Scots who had been engaged by the 'Yes' campaign, and those who had wanted to see at least more devolution, rewarded the SNP in the 2015 general election.

The most notable feature of the election was the appearance in a TV debate of the leaders not only of the three parties who had appeared in 2010, but of four others: the nationalist parties from Scotland and Wales (the SNP and Plaid Cymru), the UK Independence Party and the Greens. This undoubtedly helped some of the parties appearing for the first time in such a debate, but it did little to shift polls as regards the two parties fighting it out for first place. The issue of immigration underpinned support for UKIP, in addition to its traditional opposition to Britain's membership of the European Union. Throughout the campaign, Labour and the Conservatives frequently swapped the lead in the polls, but the balance of opinion was that no one would win a majority, and that Labour would probably be the largest party. There were fears among some voters that this would lead to the SNP exerting too much power in a hung parliament. Combined with a sense among many that the Conservatives were the most trustworthy on the economy, Labour failed to gain support where it needed to. When the results came, they showed the polls to have been wrong and David Cameron returned to Downing Street as the first Conservative to win a majority since 1992.

ONE-PARTY GOVERNMENT IN A MULTI-PARTY SYSTEM (THE 2015 GENERAL ELECTION)

	Seats	+/–	Votes (no.)	Votes (%)	+/–
Conservative	331	+24	11,334,576	36.9	+0.8
Labour	232	–26	9,347,304	30.4	+1.5
Scottish National Party	56	+50	1,454,436	4.7	+3.1
Liberal Democrats	8	–49	2,415,862	7.9	–15.2
Democratic Unionist Party	8	0	184,260	0.6	0.0
Sinn Féin	4	–1	176,232	0.6	0.0
Plaid Cymru	3	0	181,704	0.6	0.0
Social Democratic and Labour Party	3	0	99,809	0.3	0.0
Ulster Unionist Party	2	+2	114,935	0.4	0.0
United Kingdom Independence Party	1	+1	3,881,099	12.6	+9.5
Green Party	1	0	1,157,613	3.8	+2.8
Alliance Party	0	–1	61,556	0.2	+0.1
Others*	1	0	288,499	1.0	–2.5
Turnout: 66.1%					

Notes
* The one 'Other' MP is Sylvia Hermon in North Down, formerly an Ulster Unionist.

3
What is British politics?

What is British politics? This is not such a daft question as it sounds, nor is it that easy to answer. For a start, although many people think of 'politics' and 'the government' as similar things, they are actually quite different. 'Politics' is the word used to describe things in which politicians get involved, but can also be used to describe wider cultural and social forces. 'Government' has a different meaning, relating to the structures and processes of how the country is governed. Politicians are not always central to this, as scholars of government tend to be interested in structures and policies, in which civil servants and other parts of the policy process are crucial. Increasingly, in the context of making and implementing policy, the word 'governance' is used to describe the complex web of processes and relationships that are involved in governing the country.

Yet if we are really to understand what most people think of as British 'politics' we also need to understand 'government' and so distinguishing between the two, especially for the beginner, makes little sense. Instead, they need to be linked, and we need to look at some of the generalities which apply to both. Fortunately, thinkers have been coming up with such generalities – or 'theories' – to explain British politics for centuries. So this chapter explores those theories which are most helpful in trying to get to grips with the patterns of British politics. In particular, it focuses on the nature of the constitution: the basic rules which govern British government.

A liberal democratic state

The broadest concept which describes the UK's system of government is that of 'liberal democracy'. This is not specifically to do with the Liberal Democrats. It is the term used to describe nation states, particularly those in 'the West', which fulfil two criteria. First, they are 'liberal', in that they have a framework of legal protection for the rights of individuals. In particular, there are restrictions on how far the state can interfere in the behaviour of individuals in matters such as speech, conscience, religion, assembly and movement. This approach means recognising that majority and minority rights/interests need to be balanced. Second, such states are 'democratic' in that the government is chosen by regular elections with a universal franchise, which usually means all men and women over the age of eighteen are able to vote. Within such systems there is democratic accountability of bodies such as the civil service, the security services, the police and the armed forces. Ultimately, elected MPs hold these aspects of the state to account.

These, however, are very broad definitions of what liberal democratic systems are like and we need to delve deeper into their characteristics to understand how they work. One useful summary outlines several other features in addition to those stated above. First of all, they are not one-party states in that more than one party is competing for political power. Second, the rules of how elections and institutions operate are clear and not changed to suit one party or another, even if the system may at times be stacked more in favour of some parties than others, such as in the case of first-past-the-post elections for the UK Parliament. Third, access to positions of power is relatively open. For example, you do not have to be born into a particular family, or be hugely wealthy, even if both may often do no harm. Fourth, pressure groups are able to influence government policy in an open way, by argument or political pressure, without resorting to bribery. Fifth, there is often some kind of separation of powers, with different parts of government exercising different roles and operating as checks and balances. This system can be seen in the USA, where the President and Congress have clearly defined powers. In the UK, the system is more complicated, but there are notionally different powers for the House of Commons and the House of Lords, even if the Commons ultimately makes final decisions and the Lords has no say on some matters.[1]

The UK's claims to be a liberal democracy are not without contest. In the nineteenth century, the UK was not fully democratic (no women, and not all men had the vote until 1918). But it was relatively liberal even in that century in terms of protection of individual rights. Moreover, in any liberal democracy there is an inherent conflict between liberalism and democracy in the context of majority versus minority rights. Meanwhile, we might well ask how democratic Britain has really been when, since the end of the Second World War, no governing party has achieved a majority of the popular vote. Instead, they have governed on between thirty-five percent and forty-nine percent of the vote. Meanwhile, there are those of a libertarian bent who argue that taxation and specifically some kinds of expenditure (such as on health and education) are a major infringement of individual rights and should be kept to an absolute minimum.

Both praise and criticisms of this liberal democratic system rest on its durability/rigidity. The durability of individual governments has also been hailed by advocates of the elitist democratic theory, most closely associated with Joseph Schumpeter (1883–1950). This approach sees democracy as being about elites competing for votes and then ruling in the interests of the people. If one takes such an approach, then it is essential that any change is quick and decisive, so that governments can get on with the business of government. Such outcomes are allowed by the first-past-the-post system in which the norm is for the government to be formed by one party which does not have a majority of the popular vote. The UK has been a model of that with there being very few occasions since 1945 when no party has had an overall majority, even though no party has ever achieved a majority of the vote.

An alternative view is that one of the major failings of post-war British government has been the fact that it has been based on minority rule in terms of overall votes. Critics of minority rule point to countries whose electoral systems usually result in a coalition, and argue that such governments are much more representative of public opinion. Germany is an example of a country which has had very stable government while also having coalitions. Such criticisms of the lack of representativeness of the UK system have been made most vocally by those in the Liberal political tradition, partly because the Liberal Party and later the Liberal Democrats have particularly suffered under first past the post. Interestingly, in 2015, the parties most badly affected by the system were UKIP and the Greens. If seats were fully proportional to vote share, UKIP would have had eighty-two and the Greens twenty-five MPs compared to one each. The Liberal Democrats would have had fifty-one compared to eight. Meanwhile it was a Conservative, Lord Hailsham, who coined the phrase 'elective dictatorship' in 1976 to describe the amount of power given to a party that secures around forty percent of the popular vote.

The Westminster model

We also need to note that the UK is a particular type of liberal democracy. It is particular because it is parliamentary rather than, for example, presidential. The government (with the main ministers sitting in the Cabinet) is drawn from the ranks of Parliamentarians and needs to maintain the support of Parliament. All ministers are members of either the Commons or the Lords and when the PM wants to make ministers of people who are outside Parliament, s/he rapidly makes them members of the Lords so that they can be held accountable at least through questions from other members of the Lords. That contrasts with the USA where those who head government departments (Secretaries of State) can be drawn from anywhere but are constitutionally prevented from being members of Congress, the body (divided into the House of Representatives and the Senate) in which elected representatives sit. The President makes nominations with the Senate having to approve them by simple majority vote.

Not only is the link between the legislature very different in the USA compared to the UK, but so too is the influence of party. For example, when Barack Obama became President in 2009, he kept his Republican predecessor's Secretary for Defense, Robert Gates, in office. Gates had served not only in George W. Bush's administration, but also that of the previous President Bush.[2] This is unusual in the USA, but it would be difficult even to imagine in the UK. There have been examples of independent 'experts' being appointed as members of the House of Lords and becoming ministers (such as Digby Jones in 2007–8 as Minister for Trade), but they are rare examples and unlike the USA, such people have to become a member of Parliament (in this case the Lords) before they can serve as ministers. The furthest any PM is likely to go in the UK is in following Gordon Brown in bringing in people from other parties as advisers.[3] He did this when he first became PM with people such as Conservative MPs Patrick Mercer (on homeland security) and John Bercow (on children with learning difficulties), and Liberal Democrat MP Matthew Taylor (on rural housing). A number of 'peers' (the generic terms for male Lords and female Baronesses) from other parties also acted as advisers. However, bringing such people into the Cabinet would be unthinkable in the UK unless there was a formal coalition government as there was in 2010–15.

Moreover, the UK is not federal in the way that Germany is. Although there are many different levels of government in the UK, such as devolved assemblies or local councils, Parliament could abolish any of them by a simple Act of Parliament. In contrast, in federal countries such as Germany, the different levels are enshrined in a constitution which is much harder to amend. Indeed, most countries have a written constitution of some kind – a document where the main constitutional laws are all in one place. It is not quite the case that the UK does not have a constitution, as is often said, nor that it is unwritten. Instead, it is not written in one place and is said to be 'uncodified' – it is not a single legal code.

CONSTITUTIONS

A constitution is a document or body of law which embodies the most basic laws relating to how government operates. Most countries have a single document which is described as a 'Constitution'. These documents vary in scope and detail. Commonly, they define the powers of government, and rules relating to elections. They can contain details of the rights of citizens. They also include provisions for changing the constitution, and it is always harder to do that than pass laws which do not relate to the basic rules of government. The theory underpinning this is that any change to such rules should have more support than just a simple majority. The UK is unusual in that its constitutional rules are not contained in one single document and are instead found in acts of Parliament which have been passed over time. Consequently, the basic rules of government in the UK can be changed by a majority in Parliament or, in some cases, by the actions of a minister.

The name often given to the British type of liberal democracy is the 'Westminster model', named simply after the part of London which houses Parliament. The model covers a number of common features of liberal democracies, but also focuses on specific aspects more unique to the UK. In particular, it means a unitary state (one in which ultimate power rests in a central Parliament, rather than in any federal structure). It also covers features such as strong party discipline and strong Cabinet government. Meanwhile, a key element of the Westminster model is a permanent and non-political civil service.

So what formal rules govern this Westminster model? What, where and why is the British constitution which provides such rules? The most important point to note here is that it has evolved over the last 800 or so years and continues to evolve. There are many dates, events and laws which are crucial in the development of the constitution, but we can trace the first legal guarantee (since the Norman Conquest) that some people other than the monarch had rights back to 1215 when King John agreed the *Magna Carta* (Great Charter). That recognised the rights of barons, but nobody else.

Over the period 1296 to 1306, Edward I established the convention of the monarch summoning Parliament when he wanted to raise taxes. Conflict over the relative powers of Parliament and Charles I led to the English Civil War of 1642–9 and, briefly, the existence of a Republic in 1649–60. Although the monarch was restored in 1660, the conflict was not properly resolved until the 'Glorious Revolution' of 1688–9, during which the Bill of Rights was conceded by Mary II and William III. This established powers which remain central to the relationship between Parliament and monarch today, essentially vesting sovereignty in Parliament. The Bill of Rights formalised the convention that the monarch could not raise taxes other than through Parliament, which had been the most significant issue at stake in the English Civil War. The Bill guaranteed that there could be no restriction of free speech in Parliament and that any standing army could only be kept with Parliamentary consent, which meant that the monarch could not legally raise an army to fight against Parliament as Charles I had done in 1642. The Bill of Rights was followed in 1701 by the Act of Settlement, which prevented the monarch from dismissing judges; this had the effect of making the judiciary more independent. At the same time, the Act said that the monarch could not be or marry a Roman Catholic, a rule which was only repealed in 2013 (though the monarch must still be a member of the Church of England).

The major constitutional developments of the nineteenth and early twentieth centuries saw the vote extended to a greater number of men, with expansions of the franchise in 1832, 1867 and 1884. This work was continued in the Representation of the People Act of 1918, which gave the vote to all men over the age of twenty-one, and women over the age of thirty, thus giving women the vote for the first time. In 1928, the voting age for men and women was equalised at twenty-one, and then lowered to eighteen in 1969. Meanwhile, the relative powers of the House of Lords and House of Commons were amended. Prior to 1911, the Lords could block anything from the Commons which it did not like. This was a major barrier to radical reforms proposed by the Liberal government of the time, and in 1911 it successfully limited the powers of the Lords through the Parliament Act. This removed from the Lords any power over financial bills, which meant it could not block taxes. The Act also restricted its power to delay other legislation to only three years. In 1949, a further Parliament Act reduced the power to delay to just one year. A further major change affecting Parliament was made under the coalition government with the introduction of fixed-term parliaments. Prior to the passage of the Fixed-term Parliaments Act (2011), an election could be called at any time by the monarch, effectively acting on the wishes of the Prime Minister, with the proviso that there must be a parliamentary election at least every five years. However, the 2011 Act brought in the assumption that there would only be an election every five years unless one of two circumstances arises: two thirds of MPs vote to hold an election, or MPs pass a vote of no confidence in the government, without there being a later vote of confidence (for example, in a new Prime Minister or coalition) within fourteen days. This has removed a significant weapon in a Prime Minister's armoury, namely, the ability to call an election when s/he feels s/he is most likely to win one.

In the last twenty years, the most significant constitutional legislation has dealt with devolution and the rights of individuals. Indeed, since 1997, there has been so much constitutional change that Vernon Bogdanor sees the changes since then as replacing an 'old' constitution with a 'new' one,[4] even if the change has been through individual pieces of legislation rather than the introduction of a single constitution.

As regards individual rights, the law of *Habeas Corpus* (see p. 62), restricting the right of the state to detain people without trial, has been steadily weakened by, for example, the Prevention of Terrorism Act 1974 and the 2001 Anti-Terrorism, Crime and Security Emergency Act. However, on the other side of the rights equation, the Human Rights Act of 1998 came into effect in 2000. It incorporated the European Convention on Human Rights (ECHR) into British law, making it possible for extensive rights included in this to be enforced by a British court. Among other things, it abolished the death penalty in the UK. This had been formally abolished for murder in Great Britain in 1969 (although it had been suspended from 1965) and Northern Ireland from 1973. But it had remained in force for treason until 1998 and was only abolished for some military offences under the terms of the Human Rights Act from 2000.

Sources of the constitution

This story of constitutional evolution illustrates how far we need to look to various sources to answer the question 'What is the constitution?' The simple answer is that it permeates several aspects of British and European law, as well as the layer upon layer of established practice of government over centuries. These are so informal and flexible in their definition, that the ways in which political scientists define them vary considerably. For example, in four of the most commonly used undergraduate textbooks, writers choose between four and six main sources of the constitution, but they do not all cover the same ground.[5] This means that we can identify at least seven different significant sources which are commonly cited.

The most obvious source is statute law. These are major acts of Parliament which override other laws, such as *Habeas Corpus* of 1679, which constrained the right of the state to detain people without trial, and the European Communities Act 1972. Political scientist Michael Moran subdivides statute law into 'normal' and 'super' statutes. While both are capable of being repealed by the same process, there are some he believes would not be repealed except in the most dramatic of situations. These include, for example, the European Communities Act, and the legislation which established the Scottish Parliament and the National Assembly for Wales.

The second source of the constitution is other law shaped by the courts and judges. This is usually talked of as 'common law' or 'case law' and reflects the power courts have to determine how law should be implemented. In particular, free speech has been protected in this way. The third legislative source of the constitution is the European Union. Most recently, this has covered matters such as workers' rights, and where there is a conflict between British and European law, the latter takes precedence.

The other sources of the constitution relate to specific institutions. The royal prerogative gives the monarchy the power to dissolve Parliament and appoint ministers, although in reality, even these powers are heavily constrained. Rules governing the role of Parliament have grown up through commentaries which are taken as being authoritative interpretations of how that body should operate, most notably Erskine May's *A Treatise Upon the Law, Privileges, Proceedings and Usages of Parliament* (1844). Other commentaries have been influential at different times, such as Sir William Blackstone's *Commentaries on the Laws of England* (1765–9), Walter Bagehot's *The English Constitution* (1865–6) and Albert Venn Dicey's *Introduction to the Study of the Law of the Constitution* (1885). Related to the contents of commentaries are Parliamentary conventions which have meant that for almost the entire twentieth century, it has been assumed that Prime Ministers must be members of the House of Commons. Previously, they were regularly drawn from the Lords.

Finally, Michael Moran argues that there are broad cultural limitations which constrain lawmakers significantly. In particular, these have affected the franchise and which people should have it. It is currently defined by age, but has in the past applied different ages for men and women, or not given any women the vote, or only allowed men to vote if they owned or rented a certain amount of property. These limitations may sound ridiculous now, but in their time they were no more controversial than an age restriction is now.

The result of all these sources is not so much that the constitution is unwritten, because it is largely written, but rather that it is not codified into one constitutional document. Moreover, because law that is constitutional does not require special ratification as it does in other countries, governments have much power to alter it.

Would it make any difference if Britain's constitution were written down in one document, and how might it happen? Most other countries have some form of codified constitution setting out the basic rules of government and there is growing support in the UK for the idea that one might be useful for us too, not necessarily as a means of changing the role of government, but simply as a way of making it clear who does what.

Most constitutions have arisen from a period of change, often revolutionary. The American constitution was drafted at a time when the country had just thrown off British rule for misuse of power, and Americans wanted to avoid such abuses happening again. The current German constitution followed very different abuses of power in 1933–45 during which time constitutional law had been ignored by the Nazis. However, despite there having been some kind of revolutionary change leading to a constitution being drafted for the UK, the process of doing so is likely to involve one feature common to the early stages of all constitutions: the holding of a constitutional convention consisting of representatives from across government and society to try to ensure that any document has as much support as possible.

Once agreed, a constitution's greatest advantage would be in defining very clearly how the most fundamental laws of the nation, such as those dealing with civil liberties, could be changed. It would be likely to include a requirement that they could only be amended with more than a bare majority in the legislature. It is common for a two-thirds majority to be required for such major changes and that offers significant protection against the predilections of temporarily dominant 'majorities' (which may often only have the support of about forty percent of voters). Whether that makes it hard for the country to be governed in a time of crisis is something that would have to be debated before adopting a codified constitution.

Governance

Some recent work on British government sees the idea of the Westminster model as quite limited in that it only describes a small part of the system of government. Such writers use the term 'governance' to describe how British government works today. Work on the Westminster model has focused on formal structures and laws. Underpinning this has been a sense that there are some fairly easy to understand processes which explain how government works, whether or not one thinks they are effective. However, the emergence of the concept of governance in the early part of the twenty-first century is a useful way of looking at the way in which the structures of government operate in both formal and informal ways.

Work on governance is associated with a number of academics such as Rod Rhodes, Mark Bevir, David Marsh, David Richards and Martin Smith.[6] Linking their work together is a sense that government is now about so much more than what goes on in central institutions. Instead, they believe that power now lies in many different places. Some work on governance focuses on the importance of networks which give newspaper editors or special advisers as much or more power than all but a handful of political actors. For example, it is widely known that the strength of the Murdoch-owned newspapers was a barrier to Tony Blair trying to take Britain into membership of the Euro in the early days of his first term of office. So if one wants to understand how Blair made decisions on whether or not to enter the Euro, one has to appreciate that the pressures on him came from sources well beyond Westminster. Blair (and Gordon Brown) did not simply discuss policy earnestly with appropriate advisers in government departments such as the Treasury, make a decision and then debate it in Parliament. Instead, they had to be aware of much wider pressures on government, such as the media. In this, the views of Rupert Murdoch, even though the media is well outside the traditional Westminster model, were more important than most people inside the system. Understanding such pressures and influences is a crucial part of the concept of governance.

The theory also has much to say about government structures which may appear on the surface to be part of a traditional

model of decision making. In particular, although departments still make policy and present it to Parliament, they are
increasingly reliant on informal bodies for input to policy. The
existence of task forces and advisory groups has a much greater
impact on central government than ever before.

Finally, governance is an increasingly relevant concept in a
country where power is no longer even theoretically centred
on the Westminster Parliament. The fragmentation of political
power has been formalised with the establishment of elected
national bodies in Cardiff, Belfast and Edinburgh. Where once
Westminster dominated, it now has no power on swathes of
policy as devolution has been introduced. That is one of the
main reasons that the governance approach to the study of
British government now has very significant support among
political scientists.

4

Layer upon layer: the structure of British government

Different levels of government, and their responsibilities, have grown up in a haphazard fashion over time, sometimes with little thought about how they interact and what their relative powers are. We now have a situation where there are as many as eight different levels of government in the UK (European Parliament, Westminster, Edinburgh/Belfast/Cardiff, one English regional assembly, county councils, borough councils, town councils and parish councils), with many people having the opportunity to elect representatives to several of the levels, using different electoral systems. This chapter explores how these different levels of government operate, how we elect people to them, and how they fit together into this multi-layered system. It is a system which, as the 2014 Scottish referendum showed, contains within it the potential for radical change and even the possibility of the end of the United Kingdom as we know it.

Europe

The overarching structure within which British government operates is that of the European Union. Originally known as the European Economic Community, Britain joined from 1 January

1973. Under the terms of the 1972 European Communities Act, which the UK Parliament passed to bring about British entry, Parliament became partially subordinate to European law. This does not mean, as some suggest, that Europe has control of all aspects of British law. However, where Europe has a responsibility for an issue – under terms agreed by Britain – British law cannot be contradictory.

THE EVOLUTION OF THE EUROPEAN UNION

1957: The European Economic Community (EEC) is formed, under the Treaty of Rome, to encourage economic and agricultural cooperation between six member states: France, Belgium, the Netherlands, Luxembourg, Italy and West Germany.

1973: The UK joins, along with Denmark and the Republic of Ireland.

1981: Greece joins.

1986: Portugal and Spain join.

1992: The EEC becomes the European Union (EU) under the Treaty of Maastricht.

1995: Expansion in western Europe ends when Austria, Finland and Sweden join, making fifteen members in total.

2004: Following the development of former members of the Soviet bloc, the EU expands eastwards when the Czech Republic, Latvia, Lithuania, Estonia, Hungary, Poland, Slovakia and Slovenia join. At the same time, Malta and Cyprus enter, taking membership to twenty-five states.

2007: Bulgaria and Romania join.

2013: Croatia joins as the twenty-eighth member.

The European Union began as an economic and agricultural organisation, encouraging cooperation in these areas between the original six members who signed the Treaty of Rome, which set up the European Economic Community. As of April 2016 there are twenty-eight members whose role in the EU is governed by several treaties. Membership could rise with more countries seeking membership (Albania, the Republic of Macedonia, Montenegro, Serbia and Turkey).

Three treaties have been most important in expanding the EU's role. The Single European Act of 1986 created a single market in capital, labour and goods to try to ensure that trade in each country took place on similar terms governed by similar rules. The Maastricht Treaty of 1992 transformed the EEC into the European Union, with common citizenship through which citizens of any EU member state have the same basic rights throughout the EU. It established a single currency (which became the Euro) and the European Central Bank. It regulated working conditions through the Social Chapter, which guaranteed, for example, maternity leave rights. A Cohesion Fund was established to help projects in poorer regions of the EU. In 1997, the Treaty of Amsterdam established greater cooperation on foreign and defence policy, and common rules on immigration and citizenship.

There are six key institutions in the EU. The first two of these bodies are intergovernmental in that they involve negotiations between ministers of national governments. The European Council is a meeting of heads of government four times a year to discuss issues of shared concern. The Council of Ministers is a meeting of foreign affairs ministers and those covering any specific policy under discussion. In this body, since the Maastricht Treaty, there has been an extension of the system whereby some decisions can be made without all countries agreeing to them, where once unanimity was required. This is known as 'qualified majority voting'. A qualified majority in EU terms involves the support of fifty-five percent of member states, which must include at least fifteen of them, and those fifteen must also represent at least sixty-five percent of the Union's population.

The Council is one of the two legislative bodies of the EU, the other being the European Parliament, to which citizens of countries directly elect MEPs (Members of the European Parliament). The most common way of producing legislation in the EU is for the Council and the Parliament to agree to the law. That process is known as 'codecision'. However, neither body can initiate legislation. That role is for the Commission, which is appointed by the governments of member states, with one Commissioner per member. The Commission also scrutinises member states on how far they are implementing EU policy, and leads on international negotiations such as trade. This is the most controversial body because it is like a Cabinet in a member state, taking the lead in developing policy.

Two other bodies, the Council of the European Central Bank and the European Court of Justice (ECJ), are more specialised. The former manages the operation of the Euro and includes the governors of the central banks of those countries in the Euro. The latter is the ultimate court of appeal for matters relating to EU law, with one judge from each member state. The ECJ was crucial in confirming the relative roles of British and European law in the 1990 Factortame case. Factortame, a Spanish fishing company, appealed against restrictions on fishing in UK waters. The European Court of Justice gave an injunction against Britain's Merchant Shipping Act 1988 which had imposed the restrictions. The House of Lords ruled against the ECJ but had to refer the decision back to the ECJ as it related to EU law. The ECJ ruled that British law contravening EU rules could be struck down.

The end result of this system of European governance is a range of different rules which have different levels of authority. Regulations are legally binding. Directives are legally binding but with flexibility over implementation. Decisions are binding on those to whom they are specifically addressed. Recommendations and opinions are merely for guidance. As a result of the various treaties, these rules cover a wide range of areas, including the Euro, social policy (such as rules on equal pay), regional aid, consumer affairs (such as food labelling and the ban on tobacco advertising on TV), farming and fishing (especially the protection of fish stocks), the environment (such as water standards), and aspects of foreign policy (such as international trade tariffs).

Parliament

Despite the overall authority of Europe, most laws affecting most people on most issues are still determined in the two Houses of Parliament. One of the ways in which the UK is most comparable to other countries is in having two legislative chambers: the House of Commons and the House of Lords. This is known as a 'bicameral' system.

The Commons consists of 650 MPs. Each MP is elected for an individual constituency by the first-past-the-post system. Membership of the House of Lords varies. Once entirely hereditary, Lords and Baronesses have steadily become appointed by the government/monarch of the day. In the nineteenth century, the appointment of members for life (without inheritance of their title by their heirs) became more common. In 1999, all except ninety-two hereditary peers were removed from the Lords. Those removed retained their titles, but would play no further role in Parliament. The ninety-two who remained were chosen largely on the basis that they had a particularly strong record of taking part in debates in the Lords, and they were reappointed as life peers. In addition to a handful of members of the clergy and the Law Lords, the vast majority of peers are now life appointees. This change was part of the New Labour government's modernising agenda and there is now an ongoing debate over whether membership of the Lords should be by election.

Although there are countries with 'unicameral' systems, having just one legislative chamber, they tend to be smaller states, such as Denmark, Finland, Norway and Sweden. Consequently, whereas such a system has been widely accepted for the current devolved bodies in Belfast, Edinburgh and Cardiff, there is no significant support for unicameralism at Westminster. There is, however, great support for ending one of Westminster's oddities: the existence of the Lords as an unelected second chamber. This is unique in the Western world and is one of the major bugbears for those who want to democratise the British system. Even after the significant reforms to the Lords that have taken place over the last ten years it remains the case that nobody there is elected and nobody has any way of getting rid of them.

Various ideas for reform have been on the table in recent years. These range from a fully elected House of Lords to one that includes an elected element, although there are some more traditional yet largely silent people who would be quite happy if the system continued as it is now, without change. However, since Parliament as a whole has been more liable to scrutiny than ever before in the wake of the expenses scandal of 2009, the existence of an unelected body with so much power is widely held to be unsustainable. For that reason, one of the points agreed in the Liberal Democrat–Conservative coalition agreement was the election of a wholly or mainly elected House of Lords.

Much of the work of MPs is nothing to do with law-making. Increasingly, they act as a kind of 'super social worker' to whom constituents bring a wide range of problems. Typically, an MP's postbag will include a range of complaints from unpaid benefits to disputes between neighbours. Usually, the constituent will have tried other courses of action but been frustrated, and sees the MP as a person of authority who can help him or her out by oiling the wheels of slow-moving bureaucracies. Quite often, a government agency will respond more quickly to an MP's letter than one from an ordinary citizen because if an MP has taken up the case, it effectively implies an independent judgement that the constituent has a justifiable grievance. Many MPs spend much of their time on such local casework. In all the furore about MPs' expenses, a point missed by most people was that the vast majority of expenses are spent on employing staff to deal with casework.

However, in terms of the formal procedures of both Houses of Parliament, lawmaking is the primary role of members. Laws begin as Bills, mostly proposed by the government in the Queen's Speech. Individual MPs can also bring forward legislation, either as Ten Minute Rule Bills, Ordinary Presentation Bills or Ballot Bills. The time for discussion of such bills is allocated by the drawing of lots. Around 400 MPs do so, and those who come out in the top ten usually manage to obtain time to introduce a Private Member's Bill. Some important pieces of legislation have been introduced in this way by MPs, most notably the 1967 Abortion Act, put forward by the Liberal MP David Steel. There are also Private Bills, which can be sponsored by a local authority, and Delegated Legislation, through which a minister issues directives or regulations, but the vast majority of Bills are government-initiated and others only pass with government backing.

Most Bills begin in the Commons. From the 1990s there has been a growth in the use of an early scrutiny stage of draft Bills giving MPs a chance to comment on their details before they are actually published. It can allow for the more easy removal of practical problems than after a Bill has been set before the House formally. There is then a formal first reading on the Bill's purpose, followed by a debate during which those on either side put arguments for and against the Bill, often on points of detail and sometimes drawing on the particular expertise of MPs involved.

Then a second reading debate takes place on the Bill's general principles. After the two readings, it is examined in detail by one of the House of Commons' standing committees on specific policy areas. These committees bring forward amendments which are reported to the Commons, which can amend it further. After a third reading, if it is passed, it receives Royal Assent. This has not been withheld since 1707 when Queen Anne refused to sign a Bill establishing a militia (locally trained military force) in Scotland. She feared it might become disloyal.

Finally, the Bill is passed as an Act and placed on the Statute Book. At various stages, depending on the type of Bill, it will also have gone to the House of Lords for amendment and agreement. However, as mentioned earlier (see p. 60) the powers of the Lords to block legislation are very limited. For any legislation initiated in the Lords, there is a similar process, except that the Lords does not have standing committees. A wide range of Bills can be initiated by members of the Lords, often on areas of special interest to them. At the end of the 2009–10 Parliamentary session, Bills initiated by the Lords and still going through Parliament related to matters as diverse as building regulations and maritime navigation.

Committees are a crucial part of the work of Parliament. In the Commons, aside from the legislative scrutiny role of standing committees, there is further scrutiny of the work of government by select committees. Scrutiny of government also takes place in the chambers of both Houses through questions to ministers. The most notable weekly session is Prime Minister's Questions, which provides the political knockabout that makes such great viewing. Despite many people thinking that this is what goes on in Parliament, it takes up just thirty minutes of a packed week in which most debates are low-key and sparsely attended.

Some of the most lively debates, other than those on specific pieces of legislation, are those initiated by individual MPs through short 'adjournment debates' that give MPs the opportunity to raise at the end of each day's business a matter of concern to them (sometimes of interest in their constituency), with a minister responding for the government. A weekly ballot determines which MP gets to start the debate. Meanwhile, opposition parties are allocated 'supply day' debates and can raise any issue they like. These are used by opposition parties to flag issues of concern to them and to criticise the government. However, these supply days rarely result in any change in the law. A very rare exception was in May 2009 over the defeat of the government on the rights of former soldiers in Gurkha regiments of the British army to live in the UK. This Liberal Democrat Opposition Day vote saw the first defeat of the government in such a vote for over thirty years. Finally, since 1999, another form of debate for MPs has taken place in Westminster Hall, separate from the main Commons chamber. There are no votes, but debates are recorded and MPs have a chance to raise and debate issues which are of concern to them and their constituents, usually in a less confrontational manner than in the Commons itself. The emphasis is on constructive sharing of ideas and there are no votes. In the final full week of the 2009–10 Parliamentary session topics discussed included rail services in West Kent, the UK chemical industry and the Queen's diamond jubilee.

The government: executive and departments

Despite the theoretical power of Parliament, the reality is that it does as it is told by the government. Some of that is the inevitable consequence of having a government drawn from the ranks of MPs and peers. Prime Ministers are MPs themselves and can only form a government if they have the support of a majority of the House of Commons. However, at that point, the power of the Prime Minister takes effect. S/he ultimately decides who will be offered ministerial posts, which come with both influence and a higher salary. Those who consistently vote against the government when it is formed by their own party are seldom likely to be offered ministerial posts. Indeed, at times when votes are close, the government whips (MPs who ensure that their colleagues vote in a specific way) often use the promise of preferment by the Prime Minister as a way of persuading an MP to vote in a particular way. Meanwhile, it should be remembered that MPs are elected primarily as representatives of a party on the basis of that party's manifesto. So once in Parliament, MPs can be expected to vote broadly in line with the position of their party.

Despite the power of the Prime Minister, like so much of the uncodified constitution, there is very little which defines the role clearly and it has evolved over time, with holders of the post often taking starkly different approaches to the job. H. H. Asquith, PM in 1908–16, said that the post is 'what the office holder chooses and is able to make of it'.[1] Particular tasks for the PM include hiring (and firing) ministers, coordinating the overall work of government and playing a leadership role for the country as a whole. In doing this, PMs are now supported by staff at Number 10 Downing Street in the Policy Directorate, the Communications and Strategy Unit and the Government Relations Unit. Many PMs also have an informal 'kitchen cabinet' of close advisers who may or may not have the same function as some of the formal advisers. In the UK, usage of the term originated with Lloyd George, but Tony Blair was seen as a particularly keen user of a kitchen cabinet in recent years. Towards the end of Blair's time as PM, his was seen to consist of Jonathan Powell (Blair's chief of staff), Sir David Manning (his chief foreign policy adviser) and Alastair Campbell (his director of communications).[2] There have also been times when Deputy Prime Minister has been an important role. Clement Attlee was the first person to hold this post, during the Second World War, but it has not always been filled. Since then, it has sometimes been used by Prime Ministers to placate difficult colleagues. In

2010–15, it went to Nick Clegg as the leader of the smaller party in a coalition.

PRIME MINISTERS SINCE THE SECOND WORLD WAR

26 July 1945	Clement Attlee (Labour)
26 October 1951	Winston Churchill (Conservative)
7 April 1955	Anthony Eden (Conservative)
10 January 1957	Harold Macmillan (Conservative)
19 October 1963	Alec Douglas-Home (Conservative)
16 October 1964	Harold Wilson (Labour)
19 June 1970	Edward Heath (Conservative)
4 March 1974	Harold Wilson (Labour)
5 April 1976	James Callaghan (Labour)
4 May 1979	Margaret Thatcher (Conservative)
28 November 1990	John Major (Conservative)
2 May 1997	Tony Blair (Labour)
27 June 2007	Gordon Brown (Labour)
11 May 2010	David Cameron (Conservative)

But the PM's most important interactions remain with members of the formal Cabinet, which performs a function usually described as the 'Executive' in other systems of government. The Cabinet's precise membership varies, but it now usually consists of between twenty and twenty-five ministers who head up the main departments of government. It makes the major government decisions and resolves differences between ministers. It is bound by a convention of collective responsibility, whereby decisions are binding on ministers and they are supposed to support and defend them in public. Yet the government can easily bend the rules on the principle of 'collective responsibility', which is supposed to oblige ministers to sing from the same hymn sheet when it comes to government policy. In 1977, during a row over rules on European elections in which ministers seemed to be taking different positions, the Prime Minister, Jim Callaghan, said that it was acceptable for the convention to be breached. He added that it still applied, 'except in cases I announce that it does not'.[3]

Cabinet ministers also take the lead in Cabinet sub-committees, which first appeared during the Second World War and which deal with specific policy issues. Ministers are supposed to act on the principle of ministerial accountability, which dictates that they are responsible for their department even if it does things in which they are not directly involved. Despite that, there are clear examples of ministers not resigning when others might have done so, such as Norman Lamont clinging on to office when Britain was forced to withdraw from the Exchange Rate Mechanism in 1992.

The way in which the relationship between Prime Minister and Cabinet ministers works has been the subject of much debate. Many commentators see the different characters of Prime Ministers having an impact on decision making. When the more conciliatory John Major took over from Margaret Thatcher, that issue was brought starkly into focus. Major was said to allow Cabinet ministers far more latitude in their departments than Thatcher ever did, and the idea that Britain had Cabinet government rather than Prime Ministerial government became more valid. In such a system, the PM may be top dog, but they are essentially *primus inter pares* (first among equals). There was a reversal of this trend under Tony Blair. He reduced the number and length of Cabinet meetings, and spent less time in Parliament than even Thatcher. Instead, Blair favoured less formal ways of making decisions, such as bilateral meetings between ministers, and the establishment of task forces to take on specific tasks. Cameron continued this to some extent during the coalition, with a 'Quad' of two senior ministers from each coalition partner (himself and Clegg, plus George Osborne and Danny Alexander) being crucial in major decisions. Although this weakened the Cabinet, New Labour made a plausible case for the approach leading to better 'joined-up' government with more departments talking directly to each other, more often and on more issues, while in a two-party coalition it made sense for big differences to be thrashed out between senior figures from each party. Such developments in recent decades have meant that instead of the main academic debate being about the relative powers of Cabinet and Prime Minister, there is now a focus on the concept of the 'Core Executive'. This places the PM and Cabinet in a much wider context, drawing in the formal structures around Cabinet government, but also senior civil servants, the Bank of England and senior MPs. It is part of the overall concept of governance discussed in Chapter 3.

Within this Core Executive concept, the work of government departments is crucial. The number and scope of these vary. For example, matters relating to the environment were moved between several different departments in 1997–2010. Even seemingly stand-alone functions of government such as health have at times been rolled up with other policy areas like social security. The main central government departments are all headed by a Cabinet minister and have other ministers who are not Cabinet members. In April 2016, the Department of Health had six: an overall Secretary of State for Health, one minister and four Parliamentary Undersecretaries (each covering specific areas of health policy). Overall, there were 117 ministers, of whom twenty were Cabinet ministers. Not all wings of central government are headed by a minister. The head of bodies such as the Charity Commission and Food Standards Agency report to ministers but ministers are not involved in their day-to-day running. Meanwhile, Executive Agencies (such as the Child Support Agency) and non-departmental public bodies (for example, the Higher Education Funding Council for England) deal with the administration of policy.

In all departments, the senior civil servants are especially important. Sometimes described as 'mandarins', they are a thousand or so civil servants in the upper echelons of central government departments who have regular contact with government ministers. They are an unusual feature of British government in that they are in place regardless of the government, in contrast to the growing number of special advisers who are appointed by ministers as personal aides on the basis of their political views and ability to implement a specific set of policies. The behaviour of mandarins is governed by various rules and precedents which dictate that they should be permanent (surviving changes of government), impartial (staying out of party politics), confidential (not revealing the advice they have given to ministers), and anonymous (so, for example, ministers will not publicly blame individual civil servants for their failings).

Devolved bodies

Until the end of the twentieth century 'national' government in the UK meant government from London. But in 1997, in response to decades of pressure for devolution to different parts of the UK, New Labour was elected with a pledge to establish elected bodies in both Scotland and Wales.

These had previously been proposed in the late 1970s but had not secured the necessary support in referendums in both countries. In 1997, further referendums were held and both were agreed, although only narrowly in Wales. The National Assembly for Wales and the Scottish Parliament were established in 1999 using the Additional Member System of election. The Scottish Parliament is the more powerful of the two bodies. It has legislative power on most matters affecting domestic policy in Scotland, including health and education. Powers which remain in Westminster are foreign policy, Europe, defence, macroeconomics, social security, abortion, immigration, drugs and broadcasting. But the Scottish Parliament does have the power to vary the basic rate of income tax by 3p, which it has not chosen to use thus far, although by 2015 there were increasingly signs that the SNP government might do so. An eleven-person Executive is headed by a First Minister. In 2011, the SNP gained a majority in the Scottish Parliament, the first party ever to do so.

In Wales, the National Assembly was initially not legislative, primarily allocating funds from Westminster and implementing policies broadly determined in Westminster. However, since 2006 it has had legislative powers in most areas of domestic policy and now has a government led by a First Minister. Between 2007 and 2011, there was a Labour-led coalition with Plaid Cymru. In 2011, when Labour won half of the seats in the Assembly, Labour ruled alone though one seat short of a majority.

Labour made no pledges in 1997 on Northern Ireland but as a result of the Good Friday Agreement in 1998, a devolved Northern Ireland Assembly was established, with similar powers to those of the Scottish Parliament, although policing was initially held back to Westminster before being devolved in 2010. Initially, the Ulster Unionist Party and the Social Democratic and Labour Party held the key positions in an Executive based on the principle of power-sharing, which tries to give all main parties a role in government. This is a reflection of Northern Ireland's troubled history, and the rules of the Assembly mean that most issues have to be settled by a majority of people from both the Unionist and Nationalist traditions. After many false starts during which the Assembly was often suspended, the First Minister and Deputy First Minister posts are held by the largest unionist and largest nationalist parties, with the First Minister post going to whichever has the most Assembly members.

All of this, of course, leaves England with no government of its own. What is often termed the 'West Lothian Question' sees MPs from Scotland, Wales and Northern Ireland voting on matters affecting England, while English MPs have no say in reverse. Because England is so vast in size compared to the other three parts of the UK, Labour hoped that many English regions would adopt regional assemblies to redress this balance. London has done so, but when the North-East rejected an Assembly in 2004, the regional scheme was shelved and the issue of what to do about decision making in England remains unanswered. After the 2014 Scottish referendum, David Cameron pledged to ensure that only MPs representing English seats voted on matters affecting only England. But this remains a complex matter.

Local government

Because the UK is not a federal state in which the roles of specific levels of government are defined, local government exists because it has been created by central government. Consequently, its main function is to implement central government policy, including delivering services. It is felt to be useful to have this done by elected local people rather than by central government agencies because, through local elections, the needs of local people can be judged efficiently. Moreover, it boosts democracy in general by involving people in decision making. However, its powers remain very limited.

A series of Parliamentary acts since the nineteenth century have defined the way local government works. Like so much else in British government, local councils have developed over time through different pieces of legislation. Three important acts set out the basis. The 1835 Municipal Corporations Act particularly dealt with the cities which had grown during the Industrial Revolution. The 1888 Local Government Act set up county councils in England and Wales, with a similar structure applying to Ireland and Scotland. The 1894 Local Government Act revived parish councils and set up district councils.

Since the 1980s, there has been significant tension between local and national government over their respective powers. The Conservatives became very concerned that local government was a bastion of left-wing power which was going against the wishes of local people, even though that was a difficult argument to sustain when left-wing councillors had been elected. What really concerned the Conservatives was to see local councils pursuing agendas that were against the direction of national policy. London became a focus of concerns and, in 1985, the Greater London Council was abolished. In 1999, a new Greater London Authority was established by Labour alongside an elected Mayor. Ken Livingstone was the last leader of the GLC and became the first Mayor in 1999.

At the core of all local councils are elected councillors, elected by different means in different parts of the UK. They work with full-time staff (officers) to run council business. But beyond that, there is a huge diversity of council structures. In Scotland, Wales and Northern Ireland, one unitary authority covers each area. In England, some county and borough councils have pooled their powers into one body, but that is by no means the norm. In London, borough councils run social services, education, sport, local planning and waste collection, while the GLA runs strategic planning, passenger transport, police and fire services, and waste disposal. Boroughs and the GLA have joint responsibility for environmental health and highways. In English counties where there are not unitary authorities, county councils run social services, education, strategic planning and waste disposal; district or borough councils run housing, local planning and waste collection; and there are joint responsibilities on museums and art galleries, sport and parks.

Moreover, within this mix of councils is a mix of mechanisms for making decisions at an executive level. Among the several different systems, some make major decisions through meetings of all councillors, chaired by an elected mayor. But in the vast majority of councils, a Cabinet of portfolio holders (councillors with a specific policy responsibility such as education) is the structure. Councillors scrutinise Cabinet decisions, but those outside the ruling party have very little influence and spend much of their time helping local residents with specific problems on matters such as housing.

Courts and judges

One part of British government which is entirely unelected, but nevertheless very powerful, is the judiciary. Because of the way in which some British law is based on the interpretation of Acts of Parliament by courts, judges have a role in law-making. They also have a role, through the process of Judicial Review, of exploring whether public bodies have behaved in a way that is consistent with the rules which govern them.

In England and Wales, there are three main local courts. Magistrates' courts (of which there are several hundred) deal with minor crime, with around 30,000 magistrates, known as Justices of the Peace (JPs), making decisions. County courts are headed by circuit and district judges and examine civil cases such as traffic offences. Crown courts are the main criminal courts, and are composed of various judges (High Court Judges, Circuit Judges and Recorders). As for national courts, the High Court (divided into Chancery, Family and Queen's Bench divisions) deals with matters such as wills, company law, divorce and contracts. The Court of Appeal's Criminal and Civil divisions deal with appeals in all matters of law, with the House of Lords, until recently, being the ultimate court of appeal. That role of the Lords was taken over by a new UK Supreme Court in October 2009.

In Northern Ireland, the structure is similar to that in England and Wales, but with a slightly smaller role for magistrates. Scotland has a quite different legal system and therefore different courts. The Sheriff Court deals with most matters, but for more serious cases there are the Court of Session for civil matters, the High Court of Justiciary for criminal cases such as murder, and the Court of Criminal Appeal. As in other parts of the UK, the ultimate appeal for civil cases is to the Supreme Court, but criminal appeals are heard by the High Court of Justiciary.

Monarchy

From the outside, one of the most perplexing parts of the British system of government is the monarchy. The near-thousand-year continuity of the system (except for a brief period of republic in 1649–60) is certainly unparalleled, as is the extent to which (to outsiders) the monarchy seems to be a central part of our political system. In this hereditary system, succession passed from eldest son to eldest son, or if there was no son, to eldest daughter (as in the case of Queen Elizabeth II). However, in March 2015 (following the Commonwealth-wide Perth Agreement of 2011), succession became gender neutral – now the first born of a monarch succeeds to the throne, regardless of whether they are male or female. Where there are no offspring of the previous monarch, there is a clear line of succession back through the family tree, often involving the monarch's siblings, and this means that the current monarch can trace ancestry back to monarchs at least one thousand years ago.

In theory, the monarch is sovereign and has to agree all aspects of legislation before they become law. Moreover, s/he chooses who forms the government and has to appoint all ministers who are the Queen's (or King's) Ministers. Moreover, the monarch is the head of the armed forces and the Church of England, and awards honours to the nation's distinguished people. The monarch theoretically makes declarations of war, appoints bishops and dissolves Parliament. However, in reality, all these powers of 'Royal Prerogative' are exercised by the Cabinet and especially the Prime Minister, in the name of the monarch. As we saw earlier, no Parliamentary Bill has been rejected by the monarch since 1707, but even before then, under the terms of the Bill of Rights, the monarch's powers had been seriously constrained on matters such as taxation.

Meanwhile, in all the areas beyond the Royal Prerogative, where the monarch theoretically exercises power, s/he does so heavily constrained by convention. For example, in determining who should be Prime Minister, the monarch makes an offer to the leader of the largest party in the House of Commons. That usually happens after a general election, but where a leader stands down mid-term, his/her elected successor is invited. When Gordon Brown was elected leader of the Labour Party after Tony Blair stood down, there was no question of the monarch deciding to invite anyone else to form a government. The only circumstance in which the monarch might have any real influence on who forms a government is in the case that no party has an overall majority in Parliament. This is usually known as a 'hung' or 'balanced' parliament. In such a situation, if the leader of the largest party said that s/he could not form a government as s/he did not have enough votes to pass legislation, it is conceivable that the monarch might play a role in persuading two or more party leaders to reach agreement. For example, George V is widely felt to have played an important role in ensuring that a coalition National Government was formed during the economic crisis of 1931. In post-war Britain, there has only twice been a hung parliament: after the February 1974 election, when Labour governed as a minority until holding another election later in the year, and then in 2010 when a coalition was formed. In 2010, the monarch appears not to have played a role in encouraging a coalition. The parties were themselves willing enough to negotiate without pressure and the Queen could stand aside, simply asking David Cameron to form a government once it was clear that he had reached an agreement.

One question that is often asked about the monarchy is whether it has any place in a 'modern' system of government. Where there are other monarchies in Europe (Belgium, Denmark, Luxembourg, the Netherlands, Norway, Spain and Sweden), the King or Queen tends to have less status than in the UK. There is now pressure in Britain from some constitutional reformers such as Republic (www.republic.org.uk) for an elected Head of State in place of a monarch. Since regular polling on the question began in 1993, the move to have a republic has consistently achieved around twenty percent of public support, with around seventy percent supporting a continued monarchy, and ten percent not knowing what they prefer. Despite these figures, some polling also shows that a majority expect the UK not to have a monarchy in a hundred years' time.[4]

What are the alternatives? If one is to have a Head of State then the only real alternative to a monarch is a President, and there are broadly two types. First, there are symbolic Presidents with a largely ceremonial role and these tend to exist in parliamentary democracies where the real power lies with a figure such as the Prime Minister and the executive they head. Examples include Germany and the Republic of Ireland. They can be directly elected by popular vote, as in Ireland, or they can be elected by representatives of national/local legislatures, as in Germany. Second, there are Presidents with executive powers, elected by popular vote, such as in France and the USA. In these systems, the executive is separate from the legislature, which on the one hand ensures separation of powers and the ability to act more decisively than in parliamentary democracies. On the other hand, scrutiny of the executive can be very weak in such systems.

The challenge for those who favour a republic in the UK is thus not only to persuade the public that the monarchy is damaging and has no place in a modern society. They also have to convince people that a Presidential system is better and, if it brings with it new risks, those are ones that should be taken. One suspects that British reverence for the monarchy will take a lot of challenging.

ELECTORAL SYSTEMS IN THE UK[5]

First past the post (FPTP): Voters mark an X by the name of the candidate they support. The candidate with the largest number of votes wins. Used for the Westminster Parliament in all UK seats and in local elections in England and Wales.

Supplementary vote: Voters mark an X in one column for their first choice and, if they wish, another X in a second column for their second choice. If no candidate reaches fifty percent of the vote from first choices, all candidates except the two with the highest number of first choices are eliminated. The second choices of the other candidates are allocated to the top two and the one with the highest number wins. Used for the Mayor of London elections.

Alternative vote: This works in the same way as the supplementary vote, except that voters have more than two choices, which are transferred until a candidate reaches fifty percent. In a UK-wide referendum in 2011 this was offered as an alternative for elections to the Westminster Parliament but was defeated by around two thirds to one third in a ballot with a 19 million turnout.

Single transferable vote (STV): If applied to Westminster, each constituency would elect between three and five MPs depending on its size, with voters ranking candidates 1, 2, 3 and so on, for as many candidates as they wish. If a voter's first choice does

ELECTORAL SYSTEMS IN THE UK (cont.)

not need his/her vote, either because s/he Is elected without it, or because s/he does not have enough votes to be elected, then the vote is transferred to the second-choice candidate and so on. Used in Northern Ireland for all elections except Westminster ones, and in Scotland for local elections.

Additional member system (AMS): Each voter gets two votes. Voters get one vote for a constituency, elected by FPTP, and half the seats are elected in this way. Voters also cast a separate vote for a party. The number of votes that parties receive in this part of the election determines the other half of seats, with these seats being used to give parties fairer representation overall than they might have achieved under FPTP. So if a party wins two seats under FPTP, but should have five in proportion to its overall vote share, the first three candidates from a list determined by the party are also elected. Used for the Scottish Parliament, National Assembly for Wales and Greater London Assembly.

Closed party list: Each party lists its candidates in order of the party's preference on the ballot paper. Voters vote for a party and parties win seats in proportion to votes won. Used for European Parliament elections in England, Scotland and Wales.

So who represents you?

With parts of the UK now having as many as eight different levels of government it can be very confusing to work out exactly who represents citizens, and what they do. The answer to 'Who represents you?' depends on the issue and where you live. No part of the UK is represented by people in all levels of government, but somebody living in an English county might be represented by five. S/he might have either town or parish councillors, plus borough and county councillors, in addition to representatives in the Westminster and European Parliaments.

There are many examples of this, such as Tring in Hertfordshire, which has its own town council, sends representatives to both Dacorum Borough Council and Hertfordshire County Council, and elects members of the Westminster and European parliaments. Tring is not in any way exceptional.

In London, people have four levels of government: borough, GLA, Westminster and European. Because they will have several representatives at all levels except Westminster, there will be dozens of people to whom they could turn for help.

Within this multi-level system of governance, representatives might well be dealing with overlapping issues. For example, Michael Moran has shown how 'the humble wheelie bin' is subject to rule at several different levels of government.[6] In England outside London, rubbish collection is handled by a district/borough council. Disposal of waste is a matter for county councils, which act according to Environment Agency standards often set by central government. For some items, such as electrical products, it is the EU which sets the standards for disposal. As Moran says, this is a 'classic example of the complex, multi-layered reality of multi-level governance'. More than ever before, British citizens need to know exactly where power rests before making decisions about how to vote and where to direct complaints. However, at all levels of government, political parties are crucial, so they are discussed in the next chapter.

5

Manifestos, leaflets and members: political parties and pressure groups

When people want to change politics in the UK they have two main ways of acting. They can act alone to put pressure on elected representatives and sometimes this does have an effect. More often, they choose to organise with people of a broadly shared outlook. If they are concerned about a range of issues, they usually decide to become active through a political party to replace those who are elected and bring about change through different laws and/or policies. Yet when there is talk of British politics being in 'crisis', people are often referring to political parties. The public often perceives them as being 'all the same', which means that parties have problems in recruiting members and then persuading them to become involved. There are serious doubts over whether parties in their current form have much of a future.

Origins of parties

Why do we need parties at all? Why do we not just have a Parliament of independent-minded people who act on an issue-by-issue basis? That is certainly how Parliament once was, but over time, people have found it useful to work together with others for a number of reasons. When any group of people get together to discuss political issues they inevitably find that there are some with whom they agree more than others. They may even find that there are some people with whom they share views about most issues. To maximise the chances of these views having influence in a discussion which involves hundreds of people, like-minded people sometimes decide to work together to make the best case possible. They will also work together to try to win support from others. Inevitably, that can mean some compromise of viewpoints. People who think broadly the same on issues will be willing to surrender ground on others if it can maximise their chance of organising a strong body of opinion in favour of the position which is most important to them. Parties exist primarily because one voice among hundreds, let alone thousands or millions, is weak, but joining forces with others who share the same broad opinion can strengthen that voice.

There have also been, in any age, practical and less ideological reasons for working with others. Parliament deals with so many issues that it is impossible for each MP to keep on top of them all. Working as part of a party helps to divide up responsibilities, with different people focusing on specific issues. Meanwhile, once parties exist, they can help people climb towards the top of the greasy pole of politics. If a party is powerful in Parliament, then working up through that party can secure power within wider national politics and, ultimately, a role in government.

Party types

The key explanation for why there are parties is that they are formed around any issue or set of issues which are important to a group of people who wish to organise together. Because issues rise and fall in their topicality and importance, parties can also rise and fall. So, over time, there have been quite different party structures reflecting different issues. Going back to the early 1640s, we can see the formation of groupings within Parliament around the question of the powers of the King. These were not formal membership organisations as we would understand them today, but they were clearly organised groups.

Different divisions over, for example, the role of the Church, the balance of power between rural and urban areas, and the place of the state in social reform, affected party groupings in the eighteenth and nineteenth centuries. For much of the twentieth century, social class and views of the state's role in the economy influenced the Labour–Conservative duopoly which dominated politics from the 1920s. Meanwhile, nationalism has been a factor in some parts of the UK. The view that greater autonomy (even independence) from Westminster was the pressing concern in politics led to the formation of Plaid Cymru in Wales and the Scottish National Party. Meanwhile, in what is now Northern Ireland, politics has been divided since the 1880s over the question of whether or not the union with Great Britain should be maintained. So, for example, within the unionist parties, a wide range of views on social and economic questions are represented, which in Great Britain would lead to unionists being in different political parties. However, in the context of Northern Ireland, the union is the dominant issue and so these views are less important than they would be elsewhere.

Parties have emerged from different practical roots as well as being the result of different ideological sources. Political scientists commonly divide parties into those which are 'exterior' (or 'mass') and interior (or 'cadre'). The way in which the Labour Party developed outside Parliament from working-class movements would be an example of the former. Meanwhile, the development of the Conservative and Liberal parties in the mid-nineteenth century was largely focused on debates and individuals within Parliament and so the origins of both could be described as 'interior'.

Today, parties cannot afford to be 'interior' because they have to appeal to the public as a whole rather than focusing on events in Parliament. Consequently, parties have characteristics best described as 'mass'.[1] This involves one principal function: having a membership among the general public.

In theory, mass parties would be subject to a high degree of control by their members. Even in the Liberal Democrats, who pride themselves on their internal party democracy, there is significant autonomy for the party leader and parliamentary spokespersons, and that is even more marked in the Labour and Conservative parties. Consequently, the term 'hybrid party' is used to describe those which have the membership characteristics of mass parties, but also allow their leaders a high degree of independence on policy matters. This all conforms to what Robert Michels called the 'iron law of oligarchy' in his 1911 study *Political Parties*. This suggested that ultimately all mass organisations become controlled by an elite. A further development of this idea is the term 'catch-all party', which can be applied to aspects of the New Labour approach. It involves focusing on strong leadership in Parliament and attention to 'what works' rather than ideological concerns.

Party members

Members are crucial to parties for several reasons. First, having a membership system helps a party to communicate with supporters. Second, members are an important source of help, both financial and practical in terms of activity at election time. Third, they are a source of candidates who can take on the work of government from local to national level. Fourth, they confer some kind of legitimacy on the party outside Parliament by, at least in theory, keeping parties in touch with the general public.

Despite the importance of members, membership of the main parties is in long-term decline due to a range of deep-rooted social factors. These range from public distrust of politics, to the fact that people's lifestyles are far more diverse than in times when most men could be broadly defined as 'worker' or 'manager' and could find a party which matched that label. In the 1950s, it is believed that the Conservatives had around 2.8 million members, while Labour had around one million, with another five million notionally affiliated to the party through union membership. At the end of 2007, Labour's membership was down to 176,891 but it rose to nearly 300,000 by August 2015 (to which must be added around 190,000 affiliated union members and 120,000 registered 'supporters', who have a vote in leadership elections). Liberal Democrat membership has also fallen, from 82,827 in 1999 to 61,000 in 2015. The Conservative Party rarely publishes its membership figures, but in 2013 was said to have 150,000 members, with the Greens at 61,000 (June 2015) and UKIP at 42,000 (January 2015).[2]

Functions of parties

The modern political party has a range of functions, many of which are incredibly mundane. The first broad category of functions is related to politics on the ground in local areas. When people join a political party, while they may do so largely for ideological reasons and from a desire to change the world, the likelihood is that their initial contact will be with the local branch of that party. Indeed, they may have joined because somebody from that local party called round to see them. Due to declining membership, most local parties have a dire need of foot soldiers, so anybody who joins a party is likely to be asked at least to deliver leaflets. This is the major way in which local parties communicate with voters, and parties would like to try to deliver a local newsletter at least three or four times each year across a constituency. To pay for commercial (or Royal Mail) delivery would cost thousands of pounds for each leaflet and very few local parties have such resources.

Aside from this kind of work, which goes on all year round, there will be election-related activities with which members can help. A major task is canvassing, either by knocking on doors or phoning to ask how people intend to vote. The purpose of canvassing is to identify which voters will or might vote for your party. This information is used for several purposes. If voters definitely or probably intend to vote for your party, you will try to ensure that they actually do go out to vote by sending them a reminder leaflet and/or by knocking on their door on election day. If they appear to be choosing between your party and another, then you will send them targeted litera- ture to explain why they should vote for your party and not another. This information is related to an important polling day activity: telling. Everyone walking into a polling station will have seen 'tellers' sitting outside collecting the numbers of those who are going in to vote. Each voter has a unique number and this information is reported back to the nearest campaign office (officially called a 'Committee Room') of the party. Knowing which of your voters has voted enables parties to target its polling day 'knocking up' activities on those supporters who have not yet voted. In close elections, getting out as many voters as possible in this way can make the difference between winning and losing.

Other local activities less directly related to elections, but crucial for the money used in winning elections, are focused on fundraising. They might include quiz nights, race nights, jumble sales, wine and cheese evenings, dinners, raffles or any of the other activities which voluntary groups use to raise money. Of course, they also perform a social role in bringing together party members and might offer the chance to talk with the local MP in a more relaxed environment than usual. Social events might also focus on discussion of a specific policy matter, although people who join a political party hoping that it will be a hotbed of ideological debate are often disappointed.

Members can more easily take part in policy discussions at a national level. Although the party structures vary enormously, they do share some broad characteristics. Teams of policy specialists, sometimes led by national spokespeople (usually MPs) analyse policy on a rolling basis and propose new ideas. These teams are often heavily reliant on party members who may have professional expertise on the subject and are willing to give time voluntarily to producing reports or advising on an informal basis. Meanwhile, in all parties there is some role for the party conference in debating policy and current issues. Aside from policymaking, parties also have a national structure for running the party. Specific committees deal with matters such as finance and may also have a say in the strategic direction of the party. To some extent, they can hold Parliamentary leaders to account, or at least ensure that they are subjected to the views of members.

Parties also have a direct link to government. They provide from their ranks a source of government ministers. Meanwhile, for a population which moves around and may not have a chance to get to know a local MP, parties offer an easy to recognise brand which should be the same in different parts of the country. At the basis of this is the national election manifesto, which is a statement of what each party will do should it be elected. All parties publish one for national elections and it stands as a statement of their programme for government. It is intended to indicate what candidates will (and sometimes will not) do if elected. The manifesto of the governing party even has a quasi-constitutional status in that under the 'Salisbury

Convention' the House of Lords does not block measures proposed in the manifesto of the government. The Salisbury Convention is named after the Conservative leader in the Lords in the 1940s and 1950s. When Labour was elected in 1945 with a massive majority, it faced a Conservative-dominated House of Lords. Salisbury felt that it would be wrong to resist the will of a democratically elected government, and established the procedure of not opposing legislation based on a clear manifesto commitment.

The main political parties in Britain

In spite of these shared functions, parties are all very different. This section focuses on the ideas and structures of the two main parties in British politics, but also takes a brief look at other parties which play a role in British politics. Despite the widespread perception of parties being 'all the same' there are major differences not only of ideology but also in how they organise.

The Conservative Party

The Conservatives are sometimes known as the Tories because their origins can be traced back to the Tory Party of the late seventeenth century, which opposed attempts to exclude James II from the British throne due to his being a Catholic. The Tories were generally politically conservative and could trace their roots back to the King's supporters during the English Civil War who favoured a monarchy that was relatively powerful in relation to Parliament. By the early nineteenth century the Tories tended to be associated with opposition to political reform, and were using the label 'Conservative' by the 1830s. The modern Conservative Party emerged from a split in the

Conservatives under the leadership of Robert Peel in 1846. Peel favoured Free Trade (importing and exporting products without taxes being levied on them), but the bulk of the party supported tariffs which would protect British agriculture from overseas competition. Peelites eventually drifted towards the Liberal Party, while those who opposed Peel remained as Conservatives. For the remainder of the nineteenth century, their overall image was associated with opposition to reform and with protection of agriculture and industry, although under Disraeli's leadership in the 1860s and 1870s there were some social reforms and moderate expansion of the electorate.

The Conservative Party dominated government in the twentieth century, from 1915 only being out of office for twenty of the next eighty-two years. During this period of class-based politics, the party can be broadly characterised as that of the middle and upper classes, favouring capital over labour in industrial relations, and backing low taxes. It was also a party that was vocally strong on law and order, and tended to be more comfortable with using nationalistic symbols. None of that is to say that the party had no working-class support, nor that it was wholly against social reform. Indeed, an important element of Conservative thinking from the 1860s to the 1970s was the idea of 'One Nation', which stressed social cohesion in the interests of all. Consequently, from the 1950s to 1970s, Conservative governments presided relatively happily over interventionist social and economic policies and took Britain into the European Economic Community. However, in terms of Conservative Party members, the motivation for action tended to be to reduce the role of the state as far as possible, rather than to pursue policies which would lead to a more equal society. Members have also been enthusiastic about the more free-market policies pursued by Margaret Thatcher and John Major from 1979 to 1997 (see pp. 24–35). Although the party was seen in ideological terms during this time, it has often rejected the idea that it follows a dogma. Despite that, several thinkers have inspired Conservative politics. Edmund Burke (1729–97) and Michael Oakeshott (1901–90) are commonly cited as examples of those who made a case for gradual reform in keeping with the traditions of the nation. Adam Smith (1723–90) was an earlier free marketeer whose work is often cited by Conservatives. More recently (in the 1970s and 1980s), both Friedrich von Hayek (1899–1992), on the state, and Milton Friedman (1912–2006), on monetarist economics and free markets, have been influential.

At both the 2010 and 2015 general elections, the party characterised its approach in a way which contained echoes of the small-state Conservatism which flowed from Hayek and Friedman and provided the ideological driving force for the Thatcher governments. The Conservative manifesto said:

> [W]e offer a new approach: a change not just from one set of politicians to another; from one set of policies to another. It is a change from one political philosophy to another. From the idea that the role of the state is to direct society and micro-manage public services, to the idea that the role of the state is to strengthen society and make public services serve the people who use them. In a simple phrase, the change we offer is from big government to Big Society.

While antipathy to government was not so marked in 2015, the manifesto of that year did echo 2010 when it said, 'It is a profound Conservative belief that our country is made great not through the action of government alone, but through the flair, the ingenuity and hard work of the British people.'[3]

As ever in Conservative politics, these priorities bear the strong imprint of the current party leader. In determining Conservative positioning and policy the party leader is dominant, more so than in any other party, and this has been a feature of it throughout its history. The annual conference is very weak, with few votes taken. However, a significant body within the party is the Board, which consists of representatives from across the Conservatives and controls fundraising, membership and decisions over candidates.[4]

CONSERVATIVE PARTY LEADERS SINCE THE SECOND WORLD WAR

9 October 1940	Winston Churchill
21 April 1955	Anthony Eden
22 January 1957	Harold Macmillan
11 November 1963	Alec Douglas-Home
2 August 1965	Edward Heath
11 February 1975	Margaret Thatcher
28 November 1990	John Major
19 June 1997	William Hague
13 September 2001	Iain Duncan Smith
6 November 2003	Michael Howard
6 December 2005	David Cameron

The Labour Party

The Labour Party can trace its roots back to socialist thinkers such as Robert Owen (1771–1858) who founded the cooperative movement, which aimed to secure for workers a fair share of the fruits of their labour. Labour's roots can also been seen in the Chartist Movement which, in 1838, published the People's Charter calling for universal male suffrage, the secret ballot at elections and pay for MPs, so that not only the wealthy could be elected to Parliament. Crucially, the party's roots can be found in the trades union, which grew in strength throughout the late nineteenth century as workers in mass industries realised that their only chance of having a voice was through collaboration with others.

To some extent, the political goals of organised labour were met through the Liberal Party, but rising class consciousness led to the formation of the Labour Representation Committee (soon known as the 'Labour Party') in 1900 by four groups. The Trades Union Congress was the body representing unions as a whole and hosted the conference which gave birth to the Labour Party. The Independent Labour Party had campaigned since 1893 for socialist policies and for workers to be represented in Parliament. The Social Democratic Federation was a socialist organisation, heavily influenced by Marxism, which had been formed in 1881. The Fabian Society was a more moderate and more intellectual group formed in 1884 to argue for gradual reform through social democratic policies. Pooling their resources in 1900 represented a realisation that labour politics was in danger of being fragmented into too many competing groups and that there would be value in cooperation. This new party primarily sought to do exactly what its name suggested – represent workers in Parliament. But there was also a strong socialist dimension to its policies, with many of its members seeking radical reforms of society aimed at creating greater equality.

The initial growth of the Labour Party was helped by an anti-Conservative pact with the Liberals which enabled Labour to win twenty-nine seats at the 1906 general election. However, the Labour movement became increasingly frustrated by the Liberal Party, which was never enthusiastic about speaking for one class over another and was often ambivalent about unions. When the Liberal Party split during the First World War, and millions of working-class people were given the vote for the first time in 1918, Labour managed to become the second party of British politics.

Throughout Labour's early history, there were clear tensions which have continued to be divisive in Labour politics. Should reform be radical (socialist) or moderate (social democratic)? Is the priority to get working people elected to Parliament, or is challenging capitalism more important? Labour was in government alone twice, in 1924 and 1929–31, but was badly split over the economic crisis of 1931, and did not win a majority until 1945. It laid the foundations of post-war politics with its welfare policies and nationalisation, but for much of the post-war years was seriously divided between radicals and moderates. After one group of moderates resigned from the party in 1981 to form the Social Democratic Party, the party lurched to the left. After a heavy defeat at the 1983 election, three successive leaders (Neil Kinnock, John Smith and Tony Blair) pursued policy and organisational reforms which brought the party towards the centre of British politics. This led to the policies of the New Labour government of 1997–2010. New Labour was widely seen as having rejected most of Labour's socialist past, and to belong more in a tradition of European social democracy and the 'Third Way' which was entirely comfortable with markets in most areas of the economy and was even willing to apply them to aspects of public services.

At the 2010 general election, the party described its agenda as follows, in a foreword to the manifesto from Gordon Brown:

> The argument of this Manifesto is that to deliver a future fair for all we need to rebuild our economy, protect and reform our public services as we strengthen our society and renew our politics. We, Labour, are the people to carry out this next stage of national renewal because of our values and our understanding of the role of government: to stand by ordinary people so they can change their lives for the better. It is our belief that it is active, reforming government, not absent government, that helps make people powerful.[5]

This short paragraph sums up what Labour expected to be the key battleground between them and the Conservatives in the election: the role of the state versus the role of society. The party's 2015 manifesto was also more markedly pro-government in its overall tone than that of the Conservatives, but at the same time it presented Labour as 'the Party of equality' while placing new emphasis on 'work, family and community'.[6] The election of Jeremy Corbyn as party leader meant that much that had been at the core of Labour's approach for the past two decades would be challenged in the years to come. Through proposing, for example, renationalisation of the railways, Corbyn was aiming to place Labour on more traditional left-wing ground, and that was not something which all in the Labour Party were content with, believing that it would make Labour less electable.

Ironically, the fact that Corbyn as leader has the power to change policy comes from efforts by successive leaders to place more power in the hands of the leadership so that left-wing activists could not force their supposedly 'unelectable' policies into the party's election manifesto. The reforms of Kinnock, Smith and Blair reduced the influence of trades unions in matters such as candidate selection, and also weakened the party conference. Policy is now made through a process called 'Partnership in Power'.[7] Key decisions are made in policy commissions on specific areas, and the National Policy Forum, comprising 193 representatives, is elected from across the party. While the annual conference is theoretically sovereign, it tends to be a rubber-stamping body. Overseeing this process, and other aspects of the party's work, is the National Executive Committee consisting of around thirty members elected from MPs, unions, Constituency Labour Parties (CLPs) and other parts of the party.

LABOUR PARTY LEADERS SINCE THE SECOND WORLD WAR

3 December 1935	Clement Attlee
14 December 1955	Hugh Gaitskell
14 February 1963	Harold Wilson
5 April 1976	James Callaghan
3 November 1980	Michael Foot
2 October 1983	Neil Kinnock
18 July 1992	John Smith
12 May 1994	Margaret Beckett (Acting Leader)
21 July 1994	Tony Blair
27 June 2007	Gordon Brown
11 May 2010	Harriet Harman (Acting Leader)
25 September 2010	Ed Miliband
8 May 2015	Harriet Harman (Acting Leader)
12 September 2015	Jeremy Corbyn

Northern Ireland parties

A number of other parties are highly significant in specific parts of the UK. In Northern Ireland, parties are primarily the result of the dominance of the national question: whether Northern Ireland should remain part of the UK or become part of a United Ireland. Unionist parties support the former, while nationalist parties support the latter, although there are different approaches within the two communities. The Alliance Party is a cross-community party which believes that the national question should not dominate politics.

Within unionism, the Ulster Unionist Party (UUP) was the dominant party throughout Northern Ireland's history until the 2003 Assembly elections, when it was overtaken by the Democratic Unionist Party (DUP), which had traditionally been less willing to consider sharing power with nationalists. Within nationalism, from the early 1970s until the 2003 election, the leading party was the Social Democratic and Labour Party (SDLP) which supported a United Ireland, but only through the consent of the people of Northern Ireland. In 2003, it was overtaken by Sinn Féin (an Irish name roughly translated as 'Ourselves') which, while within the broad nationalist family, is usually described more specifically as a republican party, and also has a commitment to broadly socialist policies. Like the SDLP, Sinn Féin wants a United Ireland, but as supporters of the Irish Republican Army (IRA), its members were once willing to use violence to bring that about. However, Sinn Féin has now rejected violence and, as the largest nationalist party, shares power in the Northern Ireland Executive. The Executive is headed by the DUP with Sinn Féin taking the Deputy First Minister role. All four of Northern Ireland's largest parties have won seats in Westminster parliamentary elections, but Sinn Féin does not take up its seats as it does not recognise British sovereignty over Northern Ireland and will not take an oath of allegiance to the British monarch. In 2015, all but the Alliance Party won seats. There is also one Independent MP from Northern Ireland, Sylvia Hermon, who left the UUP in 2010. The Liberal Democrats and the Labour Party do not organise elections within Northern Ireland (even though people from Northern Ireland may join both parties), and instead they are close to Alliance and the SDLP respectively.

KEY FIGURES IN THE NORTHERN IRELAND PEACE PROCESS

Five politicians in Northern Ireland were crucial to the peace process in the 1990s: David Trimble (1944–), Ian Paisley (1926–2014), John Hume (1937–), Gerry Adams (1948–) and Martin McGuinness (1950–). All of these figures took political risks, which others

KEY FIGURES IN THE NORTHERN IRELAND PEACE PROCESS (*cont.*)

would not have taken, in order to bring about a situation in Northern Ireland in which political violence would cease, and locally elected politicians could make decisions in the Northern Ireland Assembly. In the first instance, from 1988, John Hume, the leader of the SDLP, took huge risks in engaging in discussions with the Sinn Féin President, Gerry Adams, when it was felt to be electoral suicide to talk to politicians who were associated with the IRA. Adams and McGuinness then took both personal and political risks in persuading the IRA to call a ceasefire in 1994, and leading them in to political talks. When those talks resulted in a deal which fell far short of the United Ireland for which the IRA had fought, they both took big risks again in signing the agreement. The same risks were taken by David Trimble, who, as Unionist leader, faced severe pressure from within his own ranks not even to talk to people connected with the IRA, let alone join them in government. Ultimately, it was Ian Paisley (the leader of the Democratic Unionist Party), who had been an opponent of all these moves all the way along, who took a massive risk in dropping his party's opposition to Sinn Féin and in working out some common ground with former foes. All men have at times responded to their supporters, but they were also willing to lead them, sometimes screaming and kicking, down a different path for peace.

Scotland and Wales

In Scotland and Wales, the UK-wide parties face stiff competition from the Scottish National Party and Plaid Cymru (Party of Wales). Indeed, both have been in government, with the SNP even governing on its own in Scotland. Plaid Cymru was formed in 1925, and gained its first MP in 1966. It has a stated aim of promoting 'the constitutional advancement of Wales with a view to attaining Full National Status for Wales within the European Union'.[8] However, it focuses far less on Welsh independence than it once did and tends to campaign more on social and economic policies from a broadly centre-left perspective. The Scottish National Party was formed in 1934 after two predecessor parties merged. On socio-economic questions it covers a range of opinions from social democratic to socialist, but its main aim is to secure Scottish independence within the EU. In 2011, it gained an overall majority in the Scottish Parliament, with Nicola Sturgeon replacing Alex Salmond as First Minister in November 2014. She then led her party to an astonishing result in the 2015 general election with the SNP winning fifty-six of Scotland's fifty-nine seats, a gain of fifty, mostly at Labour's expense. This came on the back of anger at Westminster's reaction to the referendum on Scottish independence, combined with a growing sense of Scottish national pride and increased support for the SNP triggered by the referendum itself.

Other parties

The Liberal Democrats

The Liberal Democrats are among the most democratic parties in the UK. The key decision-making body is the party conference, which has sovereignty on policy. Between the twice-yearly conferences, the party's Federal Policy Committee draws up policy papers for discussion at conference, and local parties (plus organisations within the party such as the youth/student group) can also propose motions for discussion. An elected body, the Federal Conference Committee, runs the conference, while the elected Federal Executive has overall responsibility for organisational matters within the party.

The party was formed in 1988 as a merger of the Liberal Party and the Social Democratic Party, which had worked together as the 'Alliance' from 1981. The SDP had emerged from the Labour Party that same year, and initially consisted largely of Labour supporters who thought that Labour had become too left-wing. The Liberal Party's roots were in the Whigs, who emerged during the late seventeenth century as supporters of constraints on the powers of the monarch. In 1859, the Whigs merged with Peelite Conservatives, those already calling themselves Liberals and some 'Radicals' and from then until the First World War, the Liberals were the dominant party of government, pursuing a range of policies to expand the franchise, allow greater religious freedom and bring about modest redistribution of income. A significant development in Liberal thought took place in the 1890s as the party came to embrace 'New Liberalism', which advocated greater state involvement in welfare policy. This ideological turn made the party into the social liberal party that laid the foundations of the modern welfare state in 1904–14. Electoral decline followed a split in the party during the First World War, partly over whether the war justified the introduction of compulsory military service ('conscription'). By the 1950s, the party was almost non-existent, with as few as five MPs, and, little more than a hundred candidates. Yet it steadily revived and, in the early days of the Alliance, looked to be a serious challenger for power. The initial merger of the Liberals and the SDP was not easy, and the party fared badly in the late 1980s until it started to benefit from tactical voting against the Conservatives, fighting three elections (1997, 2001 and 2005) primarily arguing for greater investment in public services, in keeping with its social liberal tradition. It maintained its strength in the 2010 general election, forming a coalition with the Conservatives in a hung parliament. However, such a coalition was not what most of its voters wanted and in 2015 they deserted the party in droves, its vote share falling from 23% to 7.9%, a loss of well over four million votes.

For much of post-war British political history the Liberal Democrats and their predecessors were seen as the 'third' party of British politics. From 1997 until 2010, it was very much that in parliamentary terms. However, in 2015, it was eclipsed by UKIP in the popular vote, and the SNP in numbers of MPs. Indeed, with eight MPs, its parliamentary party is the same size as that of Northern Ireland's Democratic Unionist Party. In 2014, it saw its numbers in the European Parliament fall from eleven to one, while it consistently lost local councillors during the period of coalition. Moreover, while it had not lost a single 'deposit' (the £500 payment made by parliamentary candidates in order to stand, but returned if they gain at least five percent of the vote) in the 2010 general election, it did do so in 340 of the 631 seats it contested in 2015.[9] Ranked fourth in vote share, and equal fourth in parliamentary seats, it is hard to think of the Liberal Democrats as any kind of third party. However, following the disaster of 2015 there was a surge in membership and some local election success. A Liberal party has grown twice in post-war Britain, and it could happen again.

United Kingdom Independence Party (UKIP)

A party with a claim to be the 'third' party of British politics is UKIP. Its main aim is British withdrawal from the EU, but it does also have broadly right-wing policies on other areas such as immigration, overseas aid, defence and taxation. In the 2014 European elections, UKIP came first, winning twenty-four seats and more than a quarter of the vote. In the 2015 general election, though, it secured 12.6% of the vote, putting it in third place in terms of vote share. Its leader, Nigel Farage, is popular if divisive, because he has managed to persuade people that he is not a typical politician.

THE RISE OF UKIP

UKIP's rise to third-party status has been steady since Its formation in 1993, essentially as a single-issue party campaigning for the UK to leave the EU. Its first breakthrough came in the 1999 European election when it won seven percent of the vote and three MEPs. Its first claim to be a 'third' party could be made five years later when in the same elections it won sixteen percent of the vote and twelve seats, ahead of the Liberal Democrats on vote share and tying with them on seats. UKIP moved into second place on vote share (17%) behind the Conservatives in the 2009 European elections and tied with Labour on MEPs, then came first in 2014 with twenty-seven percent of the vote and twenty-four MEPs. Despite these European successes, UKIP struggled at general elections, winning only three percent of the vote in 2010 and less before that. But in 2015, having tapped into a vein of public discontent with politics, in addition to securing a right-of-centre vote on issues such as immigration, UKIP became the third party of UK politics in terms of popular vote share. The traditional complaint of third parties has been that their parliamentary seats do not reflect their votes across the country, and this affected UKIP more than it has any other third party. Their one seat in the House of Commons in 2015 was the result of a by-election following the defection of Douglas Carswell from the Conservatives, with the seat being held in the general election.

The Green Party

The Green Party was initially known as the Ecology Party, formed in 1975. It has had representation in the European Parliament (since 1999), the devolved bodies in Edinburgh and Belfast, the Greater London Assembly and several local councils, in some of which it has taken part in governing coalitions. Although seen as a party which is mainly concerned about the environment, it has a full range of policies on other areas, which could be described as broadly left-wing in terms of promoting equality and redistribution. The peak of Green Party support thus far was fifteen percent in the 1989 European elections. Ten years on, although the party only received six percent of the vote, the introduction of proportional representation led to it winning two seats in the European Parliament, while in 2014 it won three. In the 2010 general election, the then party leader, Caroline Lucas, was elected as the first Green MP, representing Brighton Pavilion. She held the seat in 2015 and the party's national vote share went up from just 0.9% in 2010 to 2.9%. The party has gained support as a repository for votes from the left of politics. However, it is now far more established in many parts of the country through local councillors than it was at its 1989 European election peak.

British National Party (BNP)

The other minor party which has attracted some national attention is the British National Party (BNP), formed in 1982. Its primary concern is immigration, proposing, it says:

> an immediate halt to all further immigration, the immediate deportation of criminal and illegal immigrants, and the introduction of a system of voluntary resettlement whereby those immigrants who are legally here will be afforded the opportunity to return to their lands of ethnic origin assisted by generous financial incentives both for individuals and for the countries in question.[10]

In the 2009 European elections the BNP won two seats. It lost them both in the 2014 election and its general election support fell from over half a million votes in 2010 to just 1,667 in 2015 when only eight candidates stood compared to over three hundred in 2010. That stemmed from the party's internal problems and feuding, and controversies over its former leader Nick Griffin (now no longer in the BNP). It is often described as a fascist party and, while it might appear to be electorally dead, fascist parties in Britain have periodically grabbed some public attention, and a small proportion of support, since the 1930s.

Two-party politics?

The UK is widely said to have had two-party politics in that, at least since 1945, governments have only ever been led by Labour or the Conservatives. However, this view is increasingly problematic, not only because of the 2010–15 coalition. After the 2015 general election, there were representatives of eleven different parties elected to Parliament, in addition to one Independent. Simply looking at votes cast in Parliamentary elections tells us that around one third of those who voted in 2015 did not support either Labour or the Conservatives. So the extent to which the electorate is only interested in two parties is highly doubtful, and this can be seen even more clearly in European elections where Labour and the Conservatives tend to gain less than half of the vote between them.[11]

Meanwhile, even where there are two parties in competition, the two parties vary. While there are certainly many seats in which elections are a choice between Labour and the Conservatives, there are many other areas where this is not true. For example, in Parliamentary elections in Cornwall, the Conservatives compete largely with the Liberal Democrats. In many cities in the North of England, competition has been between Labour and the Liberal Democrats, with UKIP a growing force. Across Scotland and Wales Labour fight it out with the nationalist parties for first place overall. So while there may be two-party competition, which two parties that involves varies enormously.

We must also question the extent to which there is even two-party competition and whether we instead have a system in which one party usually dominates. For example, there was no serious question of anything other than a Conservative victory in 1983 or 1987. In 1997, it was certain that Labour would win, just as it was in 2001 and 2005. So for lengthy periods of time, the UK has had not two-party politics but what is known as a 'predominant party system' in which one party dominates. This is partly a function of the electoral system for Parliament, in which any party that can hold on to around forty percent of the vote can entrench itself in power. Consequently, not only is the third party out of meaningful competition, so too is the second.

Do parties make a difference?

One question that is often asked about parties is whether it really makes a difference which party is in power. There is a great deal of public cynicism about what motivates politicians, and inevitably people are disappointed by governments, if only because they come up against practical problems which they sometimes handle badly. Moreover, the accusation that parties become incorporated into a political system and end up changing little has particularly been thrown at Labour governments by disappointed activists. Such frustrations can lead to the public expressing the view that it does not make much difference which party is in power.

On occasion, one suspects that such assertions are sometimes used as an excuse for not thinking about complex questions to which the answers may not be clear. Parties cannot always offer stark choices because sometimes answers to complicated questions are themselves complicated. However, there has been much academic debate on whether parties are steadily converging or whether there is significant divergence. The classic text on the issue is Richard Rose's influential 1980 study *Do Parties Make a Difference?*

One answer to the question is that we can see several examples since 1945 of parties converging on similar policies. For example, after being opposed to much of the legislation introduced by Labour in 1945–51, the Conservatives came to accept the basis of the modern welfare state. Indeed, on building council houses in the 1950s, the Conservatives even tried to go further than Labour. As we saw in Chapter 2, the 1950s and 1960s are usually seen as a period of consensus based on social democratic values. More recently, a 'neo-liberal' consensus has taken hold. None of the main parties challenges the place that markets were given in the economy by the Conservatives in the 1980s. On issues of policy detail, New Labour did nothing to alter the position of trades unions in Britain, even though Labour MPs had bitterly opposed the union legislation of the 1980s.

However, there have been clear examples of parties changing the direction of public policy. That happened in 1945 with Labour implementing the Beveridge Report. There was no question of Labour cutting income tax had it won the 1979 election, yet it was a matter of principle for Thatcher. Had the Conservatives won in 1997, there was no question of the Conservatives spending on the NHS in the way that Labour did in government, nor would we have seen the constitutional reforms such as devolution which Labour introduced. These policies have all made a huge difference and if they had been the only issues at stake in 1945, 1979 and 1997 (which they were not) they would have marked great differences between the parties. We also saw some big differences in the 2010 coalition agreement when compared to the manifestos of the two parties involved, which suggests that two parties in government will come out with different policies than if they had governed alone.

In addition to what parties actually do, what they say about their 'ideal' world illustrates significant differences between party activists, which says much about their priorities. Labour (and usually also Liberal Democrat) activists want a more equal society and believe that the state has a role in achieving that. Conservative activists tend to be motivated by a desire to reduce the role of the state. These are significant ideological differences and if they did not exist then we would see much more movement of members between parties. These disparities point to parties meaning to make a difference. The conclusion of most academic writers is that, when in office, they do so, if not as much as they intend to or sometimes claim. Where there has been convergence it is usually followed by a period of divergence in which parties go back to their core beliefs. So whether we live in a time of convergence or divergence, we should be careful about seeing either as the natural state of politics, and instead see the amount of difference between parties as cyclical.

Are pressure groups the new parties?

Trying to deal with some of the perceived failures of government and parties is where pressure groups play an especially important role. Pressure groups in the UK can be grouped into two main categories: interest groups and cause groups.

'Interest groups' represent people who have a specific interest, quite often work-related. Trades unions, the Law Society and the British Medical Association are all examples of interest groups, along with bodies which represent those suffering from particular illnesses. These interest groups monitor government policy and try to ensure that it does not harm the interests of their members. They also try to advance their members' interests by lobbying government and parties to implement particular policies.

Whereas membership of interest groups is usually restricted to particular people who share that interest in some form, 'cause groups' aim to attract people who believe in a particular cause, whatever their expertise or interest might be. Examples include Friends of the Earth, Greenpeace and the Society for the Protection of the Unborn Child. These bodies monitor policy and lobby parties on a wider range of issues, usually from a specific ideological perspective and usually to promote specific policy reforms. In many cases, people may be involved in a cause group and a political party, but the two are different in the breadth of their concerns, with parties having a much wider remit. For example, Friends of the Earth would have policies on a broad range of matters related to the environment such as health and education, but it would not usually get involved in matters like constitutional reform or defence.

Although pressure groups are very different to parties, they can be attractive for some of the reasons that once made people join parties. They carry with them a sense of idealism and a desire for change, without the negative associations of politics and political parties. For this reason, while party membership is falling, membership of some pressure groups is steadily rising and there is no sign that that trend is going to alter.

For all the attraction of pressure groups, they fail in one crucial respect: they could not form a government. For this, parties are still needed because only groups based on a broad range of issues can hope to offer the voters any sense of what a government might be like. Imagine if people decided to elect an anti-poverty pressure group to be the government of the country. There would be no real idea what such a group would do about a very wide range of policy areas such as Europe, defence, constitutional reform, many aspects of health and education, and much of the economy. Such a group might well contain very different opinions on these issues and if it were elected on the basis of a narrow platform, then the public would soon be very shocked.

If we did not have parties, we would certainly have to invent them. I reached this conclusion when out canvassing for a local council by-election on a cold February evening in 2010. The reaction was generally very good, but quite a few people put forward the 'clear off, you are all the same and only in it for yourselves' response. In such a situation, one can point out that most of us involved in politics do it in our spare time, voluntarily, unpaid and on top of jobs and family commitments. It costs us time and money. People are often pleasantly surprised to hear that, but for some it makes little difference. After meeting one of the latter people I asked myself 'What would happen if all the parties went on strike?' I wondered 'What would happen if we said, sorry, we are going to stay at home with our families on a cold evening and let someone else worry about public services and the local community?' I rapidly came to the conclusion that some public-spirited people (those not already involved in parties) would decide that something had to be done. They would put forward policies and they would stand for election. They would rapidly find that it was hard to campaign alone, and that there were some people also running for office with whom they had more in common than others. They would start working with these people, and making compromises where they disagreed, just for the sake of having other people to continue to work with so that they could get things done. In short, political parties would be born again. Like it or not, and crisis or not, political parties are an inevitable part of the political process.

6
Policy: the big issues

The most important issues in British politics and government are dictated by the bread-and-butter concerns of voters: schools, tax, the National Health Service and benefits. Increasingly, voters are also concerned about the environment. This chapter sets out how the systems and policies relating to these policy areas have developed and how they operate now. It focuses on issues dealt with at Westminster, which increasingly relate to England alone. It begins with the economy because that underpins all other issues.

Economy

It is widely believed that policy on 'the economy' is a decisive factor in determining general election results. David Sanders, an academic expert on election results, says, 'If the public is optimistic about the economy and a government has a reputation for economic competence, the opposition party has its work cut out to win power.' Leading pollster Peter Kellner argues, 'The economy is almost always decisive in general elections.'[1]

By 'the economy', what is meant is a wide range of factors beyond simply how business and money making are faring. It has included at different times, for example, the state of manufacturing, unemployment, overseas trade, ownership of industry, banking, regulation, inflation, interest rates and living costs. In addition, when the public talk about 'the economy' they often also mean matters which are more correctly part of 'fiscal policy': the government's levels of spending and the taxes it sets to fund that. Central to public concerns are growth and public spending, but economic issues have an impact on all policy areas.[2]

Economic growth means growth in gross domestic product (GDP), which is a measurement of the value of all types of economic activity, including all employment and production. Its merits are disputed by some, not least environmentalists, who say growth can deplete finite resources, if not done in an environmentally sustainable way. However, it is part of the current neo-liberal consensus that growth in GDP is a good thing. It is said to have, among others, two particular benefits: increasing the prosperity of individuals, and contributing to the government's ability to fund public services through the generation of tax revenues. Consequently, all British governments since 1945 have sought to grow the economy and have at least partly been judged on their success at doing so. It has suited both those who wish to increase personal wealth and living standards, and those who wish to increase spending on public services. Indeed, New Labour's time in government in 1997–2010 was an example of both approaches combined. However, the economic problems faced since the late 2000s have threatened the assumption that indefinite growth is possible. The Office for National Statistics sums up the situation as follows:

> GDP in the UK grew steadily during the 2000s until a financial market shock affected UK and global economic growth in 2008 and 2009. Economic growth resumed towards the end of 2009, but generally at a slower rate than the period prior to 2008. This growth was also erratic, with several quarters between 2010 and 2012 recording stagnant or declining GDP. Since 2013, GDP began to grow again, passing its pre-downturn peak in Quarter 3 (July to Sep) 2013.[3]

As Chancellor of the Exchequer, George Osborne's explanation of such growth is that jobs have been created due to business having confidence in the government to run the economy, especially by bringing down the budget deficit.[4] This points to the second major issue in UK economic policy (or more correctly 'fiscal' policy): public spending and its effects on public debt.

When government wishes to spend money it broadly has two options: raise that money through taxation or charges (or other revenue-raising measures such as privatisations of the public sector), or borrowing. Since the end of the Second World War, the amount the government spends (total managed expenditure, or TME) has steadily risen. For example, between 1948–9 and 1999–2000 there was an average annual increase of 2.8% in spending in real terms (which means that account has been taken of inflation so that costs can be compared from year to year). From then until 2009–10 it increased at about 4.5%. In the first place that greater increase was a result of decisions by Labour to spend more on public services, but in the latter years it arose from attempts to deal with the recession, including support for the banking sector. In actual spending, using October 2014 figures as a baseline, the government spent £720.4 billion in 2013–14, which was almost exactly what had been spent in 2008–9, and was a sizeable increase on what was being spent (less than £500 billion) when Labour took office in 1997.

However, it should be noted that, because the economy was growing well over the late 1990s and during most of the 2000s, the share of GDP being spent by government does not tell the whole story. Between 1997 and 2008 it varied between 37.8% and 46.6%.[5] But not only was that a higher percentage of GDP overall, it was a larger share of a larger amount because the economy had grown. The alternative is to borrow if one wishes to increase (or even maintain) spending. And tackling the level of the budget deficit (the difference between income and expenditure) so as to reduce borrowing by government is the other key way in which public spending is measured. Net annual borrowing reached a peak in 2009–10 at over £150 billion as the government sought to tackle the recession, but declined thereafter.[6] A significant driver in this has been cuts across government budgets (except in notionally 'protected' areas such as the NHS, schools and pensions, which can still face decreases in spending in real terms). When the cuts were first announced in 2010, Robert Chote, the director of the Institute for Fiscal Studies, described them as 'the longest, deepest sustained period of cuts to public services spending at least since World War II.'[7] By 2015, the average level of cuts for unprotected government departments was 20.6% across the previous five years, with spending overall cut by 9.5%.[8]

Education

Education has changed dramatically in Britain since the Second World War. For example, prior to the war, only around 50,000 people annually were students at universities. That figure increased to over 200,000 by the 1970s and is now at over two million UK nationals, plus another 300,000 or so from overseas. Some issues in higher education have been controversial, such as the introduction of tuition fees.

However, it is the school education system that has been the most consistently emotive issue in politics. Especially in England, it plays into a wide range of debates about who we are, where we have come from and where we are going to. It involves difficult issues such as the role of the state in shaping our lives, and the extent to which parents should have choice over how and where their children are educated. Like so much else in British life, our school system is one that has evolved gradually over time, with each reform built on the layers of previous systems, which often survive in some form.

The most fundamental and controversial division within the system is between schools financed by fees paid directly by parents and those funded through general taxation. The former are known as 'public' (note the different usage of 'public' compared to the USA, where the term is used for non-fee-paying schools) or 'private' schools. The use of the term 'public' in the UK goes back to a time when there were no state-funded schools and only people who were the better off could get an education for their children. They had a choice of educating them at home with a private tutor, or sending them away to a so-called 'public' school (often a boarding school). In either case, they paid fees. Today, these schools prefer to call themselves 'independent schools', but both 'public' and 'private' are used commonly, with the former particularly used for the oldest schools such as Eton and Harrow. Although only about seven percent of the population uses fee-paying schools, they sometimes dominate debate. In some years, around half of those entering the most prestigious universities such as Oxford and Cambridge have been to such schools, and the wider public often feels that being able to afford such a school buys a better education. No government has ever tried to tackle private schools head-on, although universities are increasingly encouraged to discriminate in favour of applicants who have been to state schools.

'State' schools are those funded by the government using money from taxes. They educate around ninety-three percent of the population and are the subject of heated political debate over standards, access and structures. When politicians talk about 'schools', these are the ones they are talking about. The origins of a state system of education are found in the early nineteenth century. Prior to that, basic schooling for those not able to pay fees was provided on a fairly random basis by charity and volunteers, especially the churches. In the 1830s, a national grant system was set up to help fund schools for the poor, although the money went to local voluntary bodies.

The first major step in creating a national framework came in 1870 with W. E. Forster's Elementary Education Act. This applied to England and Wales (developments in Northern Ireland and Scotland are discussed later). It allowed local ratepayers to request that locally elected school boards be set up to assess the state of elementary education in their area. Where the board decided that provision was inadequate, schools could be set up and funded through a mix of local taxes (to pay for the poorest) and fees paid by parents. Local authorities were given the power to require all children between the ages of five and twelve to attend school, and by the mid-1870s, around half were so compelled. The act was not uncontroversial. Some ratepayers did not want to carry the costs of educating the poor, and did not see why they needed to be educated. Meanwhile, some churches that were already running schools resented interference by local government.

Over the next thirty years, there was therefore a series of Parliamentary acts which toughened up requirements, with education made compulsory for five- to ten-year-olds in 1880, state payment of fees for this age range introduced in 1891, and the school-leaving age raised to eleven, then thirteen. However, the major change in moving from a voluntary to state-run system was the 1902 Balfour Education Act. This replaced school boards with Local Education Authorities (LEAs) across England and Wales, run by either county or borough councils. They had the role of recruiting and paying properly qualified teachers. Where there were church schools in an area, these came under the LEA remit: that the churches accepted this was because in so doing they obtained local funding. In 1918, the Fisher Education Act developed that system by raising the school leaving age to fourteen, with LEAs becoming responsible for secondary schools (for children aged eleven and over).

The system in England and Wales further developed in 1944 with the Butler Education Act. This act took secondary secondary education fully into state control, with fees in locally run secondary schools scrapped, and the school-leaving age raised to fifteen. It also established the structure of schools which dominated England and Wales until the 1960s, and is still in place in some ways in a few parts of England. This was a tripartite system of grammar schools, secondary moderns and technical schools. The system was underpinned by the eleven-plus exam which children took at age eleven. This focused on academic subjects, and those who did best in the exam went to grammar schools, with most of the rest going to secondary moderns, and some to technical colleges. At grammar schools, pupils would study a range of academic subjects which could lead to university entrance. Secondary moderns taught a mixture of academic and vocational subjects, while technical schools focused mainly on vocational subjects which would prepare children for a trade. In debates leading to the 1944 Act, the government considered whether it should do anything about private schools and church schools. It did nothing about the former, but tried to bring the latter more under state control by offering them more money.

From the late 1940s to the 1970s, there were two major themes in the politics of education. First of all, although the grammar school system enabled many talented children from relatively humble origins to excel at school and get to university (this could be said of future Prime Ministers Harold Wilson, Edward Heath and Margaret Thatcher), it only ever educated a minority of children. There was great concern about children who missed out on grammar school at age eleven, but might have developed later. Consequently those on the left of politics became opposed to the eleven-plus divide. An especially staunch opponent was Tony Crosland, who became Secretary of State for Education and Science. His wife later recalled how he said, 'If it's the last thing I do, I'm going to destroy every fucking grammar school in England. And Wales. And Northern Ireland.'⁹ In Crosland's brand of social democracy, the same educational chances for all was a fundamental aspect of equality of opportunity and he set about creating 'comprehensive' schools, which taught all subjects without a divide at eleven. Instructions on moving to a comprehensive system were issued to local authorities in 'Circular 10/65' from the Department for Education and Science (DES). But the circular used the word 'request' rather than 'require' in its instructions to local authorities to end the tripartite system, partly because the DES was not directly in control of local authorities on the matter. That left considerable wriggle room for any local authority which was opposed to comprehensives. Although most did implement the request, others did not, and when the Conservatives came to power in 1970, they allowed more flexibility. When Labour took office in 1974 they made comprehensive schools a requirement, but the Conservatives reversed that in 1979. Although there was a significant switch to comprehensives in the 1970s, by the 1980s there were still many areas which had grammar schools and structures varied greatly across the country.

Meanwhile, a new system of assessing what children achieved at school had been established. In 1951, the General Certificate of Education (GCE) was established to replace the School Certificate. This had both 'Ordinary' and 'Advanced' levels, usually taken at ages sixteen and eighteen respectively, with pupils taking each subject separately. In 1965, a Certificate of Secondary Education was established mainly for use in secondary moderns. However, many pupils missed out on obtaining any qualifications because it was not until 1972 that the school-leaving age was raised to sixteen.

When the Conservatives came to power in 1979, they did so against a backdrop of debate which suggested that there were serious problems in schools. In the 1970s, those on the right had started to suggest that there was a culture of underachievement in schools and that in comprehensives there were low expectations for working-class children. One school seemed to sum up other problems: at William Tyndale Junior and Infants School in London, it was found that children were being given a great deal of choice over what they studied, if anything, and this led to the Auld Report, which criticised so-called 'progressive' education. One consequence was a call by the Labour Prime Minister, James Callaghan, for a 'Great Debate' on education. He said that there needed to be a core curriculum, overall national standards, greater parental involvement and renewed focus on the 'three Rs' (reading, writing and arithmetic).

It was to be a Conservative government which implemented these measures after 1979. From the mid-1980s, GCE 'O' Levels were steadily merged with CSEs to create the General Certificate of Secondary Education (GCSE), but the most radical step came in the 1988 Education Reform Act. This gave parents more choice over which school their child could go to (although it did nothing to create more places at the most popular schools), established a National Curriculum and introduced Standard Assessment Tests (SATs) at ages seven, eleven and fourteen. Meanwhile, reflecting Conservative fears about the influence of left-wing local authorities, schools could opt out of LEA control and be funded by direct grants from central government. Four years on, the 1992 Education (Schools) Act created league tables with which parents could compare schools, and gave a new Office for Standards in Education (OFSTED) significant powers of inspection in schools. The Major government also introduced the General National Vocational Qualification as a vocational alternative to 'A' Levels, to encourage supposedly less academic pupils to stay at school post-sixteen, and, at the other end of the age range, offered more nursery places for four-year-olds.

Despite all these reforms, debates on educational standards remained central to politics in the 1990s. As Leader of the Opposition, Tony Blair famously declared that his three priorities were 'education, education, education'.[10] His focus was on basic standards in literacy and numeracy. The 1997 Labour manifesto said that 'Nearly half of our 11 year olds in England and Wales fail to reach expected standards in English and maths.'[11] So, in the early years of New Labour's time in government, initiatives focused on literacy and numeracy hours to boost both skills in primary schools, with specific targets on both introduced for eleven-year-olds. Meanwhile, Labour brought in a maximum class size of thirty for five- to seven-year-olds, and gave schools extra money with which to recruit more teachers. There was also a focus on so-called 'failing' schools with the 1998 School Standards and Framework Act establishing twenty-five education action zones.

Labour kept many of the Thatcher/Major reforms in place, apart from bringing grant-maintained schools back under the control of local authorities. The Conservatives had encouraged some comprehensive schools to specialise in certain areas by giving them extra money if they focused on areas such as technology, performing arts, sports or foreign languages, and this policy was developed under Labour. Nursery places were greatly expanded, while in other areas Labour tweaked Conservative systems. Performance indicators such as league tables remain although they now focus more on 'value added' measures which recognise that some schools have more challenging intakes than others. SATs (in England) remain, at eleven, although they have been scrapped at fourteen and made optional at seven, while inspections by OFSTED have become more light-touch than they once were.

In the 2010 Conservative–Liberal Democrat coalition agreement, a core element of education policy was the 'pupil premium', which had been central to the Liberal Democrat election campaign but was also mentioned by the Conservatives in their manifesto. This policy had originally been proposed as far back as 2002 in a pamphlet co-written by myself and Nick

Clegg.[12] Meanwhile, the Conservative policy of 'free schools' was agreed.

As it happened, in addition to the increase in university tuition fees, both policies dominated the government's approach to secondary education, along with changes to examinations. Towards the end of 2014, over half of secondary schools had become academies, which were schools entirely outside local government control or oversight, funded directly from central government, and often involving partnerships with private schools or businesses.[13] That process revolutionises the structure of secondary education in England.

Education in Northern Ireland and Scotland

Prior to the partition of Ireland, the school system developed in much the same way as that in England and Wales, and the current school system in Northern Ireland is quite similar to that in England and Wales in terms of qualifications. However, there are two crucial differences. The eleven-plus exam persisted in Northern Ireland until 2009 only to be replaced by entrance exams for individual grammar schools. This maintained the grammar/secondary-modern divide. Meanwhile, in keeping with the much greater importance of religion within society as a whole compared to the rest of the UK, different faiths are much more closely linked to schools. In particular, most Catholic children (around forty-five percent of the population) are educated in schools managed by the Catholic Church. There are also schools which focus on the Irish language. Only around five percent of children attend an 'integrated' school, which is non-denominational in character, while the rest attend schools that are Protestant in character, though not actually run by churches. Many argue that this system perpetuates the divides which already exist in Northern Ireland, though it can just as easily be argued that Northern

Ireland is a segregated society that produces segregated schools rather than the other way round.

The Scottish system is quite different to that elsewhere in the UK. The Scottish (originally Scotch) Education Department was created in 1872, taking over control of church schools and creating a national exam board. It expanded secondary education much earlier than elsewhere in the UK, and never established state grammar schools. Primary schools run from four to eleven or twelve years old, while in secondary schools, three levels of qualification are taken, but at more flexible ages than elsewhere in the UK: Standard Grades at fifteen or sixteen, Highers at fifteen–seventeen, and Further Highers at sixteen–eighteen. The Scottish system is generally seen to be more cohesive and egalitarian than others in the UK, and fewer children attend private schools.

The National Health Service

The National Health Service is one of the most popular institutions in British society. Admittedly, people grumble about the treatment they receive, and the time they wait for that treatment. But it has been a matter of the strongest possible consensus that slaughter at the polls will follow for any politician who challenges the basic concept of a service that is free to use at the point of delivery.

Prior to the establishment of the NHS, access to healthcare depended on ability to pay, although in many areas there was charitable provision of treatment for the poor. The first step to try to deal with that problem was the 1911 National Insurance Act. All those who worked and were earning less than £160 a year, which was equivalent to about £13,400 now,[14] had to join a compulsory insurance scheme. Through four national health commissions (one for each part of the UK), they could then obtain treatment from general practitioners (GPs), and cash benefits if they were ill, but this only applied to the insured, not their families.

The proposals for a National Health Service that emerged from the Second World War (see p. 10) were revolutionary in their scope. They amounted to nationalisation of the existing piecemeal health system and offering health care for all, funded by taxes but free to use at the point of delivery. GPs worked in the same way as before, but funded by the government not patients. Although a national system, there was an element of local authority control with the establishment of fourteen regional hospital boards. The major teaching hospitals were run by governors linked directly to the Ministry of Health, thus ensuring national direction of medical training and standards. Nye Bevan, who led the introduction of the NHS, rightly said in October 1948 that 'This is the biggest single experiment in social service that the world has ever seen undertaken.'[15]

Support for the NHS soon became a matter of political consensus. Ten years after its foundation, the senior Conservative Iain Macleod said, 'The National Health Service, with the exception of recurring spasms about charges, is out of party politics.'[16] Under every Labour and Conservative government, spending has grown in real terms over the course of each government. Despite that, because it was Labour that set up the NHS, it has traditionally been Labour which is seen as the party most capable of running it, even when it is doing badly in all other types of opinion poll.

However, the basic principle of the NHS being completely free to use was undermined from an early stage. In 1951, in the face of many different pressures on the budget (see p. 10), charges for false teeth and spectacles were introduced by Labour. The Attlee government also brought in a small charge for prescriptions, although it fell to the Conservatives to implement it. Consequently, the level and scope of prescription charges became, as Macleod said, a recurrent political issue, but other charges, such as those for staying in hospital, were rejected by both parties. Labour briefly scrapped prescription charges in 1964–8, but they have otherwise remained in place.

Aside from simply running the NHS, the Conservatives developed it. Health Minister, Enoch Powell's 1962 Hospital Plan set up new hospitals across the country, to deal with the fact that none had been built since the end of the war and facilities were beginning to show their age.

By the 1970s, a number of problems were emerging in the NHS. Due to the very positive facts that people were living longer (partly because of the NHS) and there were newer treatments available, demand for healthcare was on the increase. More people wanted more treatment and for longer, and even though the amount spent on the NHS steadily increased, it did not keep pace with demand.

There were also concerns that the NHS was neither well managed nor accountable to patients and/or local people. In the 1970s and 1980s this led to a series of reforms, which sometimes left NHS staff feeling that they were in a state of permanent revolution. In 1974–9, regional and area bodies were given new roles, while advisory committees and community health councils were set up, with members nominated by local councils and voluntary organisations.

But in 1982, the Conservatives replaced areas with districts and then introduced a series of managerial reforms to implement the Griffiths Report. This had claimed that 'if Florence Nightingale were carrying her lamp through the corridors of the NHS today she would almost certainly be searching for the people in charge.'[17] New 'general managers' were given control of 'management budgets' with the aim of securing better value for money in order to release funds for other patient services.

Partially as a result of these reforms, the 1990 NHS and Community Care Act introduced an 'internal market' into the

NHS. This sought to give money to GPs, who would then purchase services for their patients from the NHS. Not all GPs opted to become such 'fundholders' and the system led to fears that there was a two-tier NHS which was on the path to privatisation.

When Labour came to power in 1997, its priority was to pump money into the NHS on the basis that it had been starved of the resources it needed as compared to other European countries. The extra money was used to provide better pay for staff, employ more medical staff and open new facilities as set out in the 2000 *NHS Plan*. However, in some areas 'rationalisation' of services led to closure of wards, which left local people in such areas wondering what happened to all the money that went into the NHS.

As regards structures, a key point is that since devolution in Scotland, Wales and Northern Ireland, the elected bodies in these countries have gained significant powers over the NHS, even though it remains funded on a UK basis. They have their own systems for ensuring local accountability overseen by elected representatives, which is much more manageable on a national basis in countries which are so much smaller than England.

In terms of the NHS in England, despite the controversies of the 1980s, the purchaser–provider split of the internal market has become accepted by the main parties and Labour did not remove the principle from the system after 1997, although it did attempt some streamlining by reducing the number of transactions which took place. That was primarily done through the establishment of primary care trusts (PCTs, often of county size) and strategic health authorities (SHAs, initially twenty-eight in number but later reduced to ten regions).

However, a new structure for the NHS was legislated for by the coalition in 2012. Through the Health and Social Care Act, both these bodies were scrapped. PCTs were replaced by clinical commissioning groups (CCGs). These are made up of general practitioners and operate across communities of various sizes: for example, a CCG could cover a whole London borough, or it might just cover part of a county. CCGs commission services from a range of sources, from NHS hospitals to private or charitable providers. SHAs were not directly replaced but upper-tier local authorities (which are generally unitary or county councils) now have a Health and Wellbeing Board which aims to link up services and holds some democratic oversight of the local NHS. Public Health England was set up to provide some national coordination of the NHS, while Monitor provides national oversight.[18] The changes by the two coalition partners were extremely controversial in Parliament, not least because they were said to be 'privatising' the NHS, with Monitor being given a role to tackle any prevention of competition within the system. Meanwhile, the coalition acted on a pledge to increase NHS funding year on year. It did do so in real terms, but only if the effects of an ageing population on NHS budgets are not included.[19]

Welfare

The social security budget (which covers, for example, unemployment benefits and pensions) is the largest single area of government spending. In 2013–14, 29.3% of the government's total spending was on social security, with the next largest amounts being 18.1% on health and 12.6% on education. Within the social security budget, spending on pensioners has for decades been around half the amount.[20]

Provision of some kind of community help for the poor is one of the longest-standing forms of collective action. A series of Parliamentary Acts in 1572, 1576 and 1597 set up a system known as 'relief' for the poor on a parish basis. It was paid for by local taxes and the rules said that those receiving payments had to carry out some form of work or be put in 'houses of correction'. The Poor Law Act of 1601 made that system national. By the eighteenth century, the 'workhouse' was at the core of the system. It provided both accommodation and a source of very menial work, along with rough living space in a 'poorhouse' for those unable to work.

By the 1830s, some had become concerned that workhouses were rather generous in their facilities, although nobody making those arguments would have chosen to live in one. Setting the tone for many criticisms of benefits over the next two centuries, it was suggested that scroungers were exploiting the system to avoid providing for themselves. Consequently, the Poor Law Amendment Act of 1834 toughened the regime. Yet, whatever the conditions of workhouses, it was the stigma of being in one which made the vast majority of people, however poor, want to avoid them.

Around the turn of the twentieth century, pressures for a new approach to the poor were coming from a range of sources. Seebohm Rowntree's 1901 report on living conditions in York shocked many with the horror of poor people's day-to-day lives. While he saw evidence of 'secondary' poverty (as a result of people wastefully spending adequate earnings, especially on alcohol), he saw much evidence of 'primary' poverty: people working hard, and living frugally, but simply not earning enough to sustain any kind of decent life. Meanwhile, those recruiting for the British Army during the South African War of 1899–1902 were horrified by the physical condition of men who were unfit to be soldiers despite having the spirit to volunteer. People from across politics began to subscribe to ideas of 'National Efficiency' which sought to improve the physical and social conditions of the people partly on the basis that an unhealthy and ill-fed workforce was economically inefficient. That argument was also made by some New Liberals, but they also focused on the moral dimensions of gross inequality, and argued that it was time for the state to take action.

From this intellectual ferment emerged a series of welfare measures when the Liberals swept to power in the landslide election victory of 1906. They introduced the Workmen's Compensation Act (1906) to provide compensation for those injured at work. The Old Age Pensions Act (1908) established (non-contributory) pensions for the poorest over seventy. Labour Exchanges were set up in 1908 to provide help for the unemployed to find work. The 1911 National Insurance Act established both health insurance schemes and unemployment benefits.

Between the wars, this system was steadily expanded. In 1925, under the Conservatives, the Widows, Orphans and Old Age Contributory Pensions Act extended the scope of state pensions, while workhouses were phased out in the 1929 Local Government Act. In 1934, under a Conservative-dominated coalition government, the Unemployment Assistance Board was set up to extend earlier benefits.

Two principles were at the heart of this system. Means-testing meant that people only received benefits if they could prove they did not have other means (which made many feel that benefits were actually a form of charity with a stigma attached). Meanwhile, benefits were often dependent on having made a contribution. In contrast, the system proposed by William Beveridge in 1942 was a universal system in that it covered all people. However, it still contained elements of selection or means-testing. Child benefits initially applied only to second and subsequent children (but were later expanded to cover all children in 1975). There was still a contributory element in that people who contributed to National Insurance would be entitled to benefits which were higher than the National Assistance paid to others. The new pension scheme that was established was also contributory, with only a safety net for those who had not contributed.

In the post-war years, amendments were made to the system. The 1959 National Insurance Act allowed people to top up their pensions with extra contributions. That was replaced in 1975 with State Earnings Related Pensions. In an effort to reduce the costs to the state of pensions, people were able to opt out of that if they were contributing to a private pension scheme.

Up to the 1980s, the rate of the state pension had risen in line with earnings, which go up faster than prices. However, that link was broken by the Conservatives in 1980 and, as a result, pensioners' incomes steadily fell behind relative to those of wage earners. By the 1990s, 'pensioner poverty' had become a part of political discourse.

The Conservatives also made significant changes to other benefits in the 1980s. Across the board, most benefits were either frozen or reduced. The Conservatives believed that people should be encouraged to make greater provision for themselves through savings or private insurance schemes which could be used in times of need, and also felt that benefits were generous enough to discourage people from working.

While out of office, Labour opposed these changes vociferously, yet in government in 1997–2010 it was faced with a rising pensions bill (as the population lived longer) and shared some concerns about benefits encouraging the feckless to avoid work. One solution found by Labour was to make disability benefits harder to claim, arguing that some who claimed them were actually capable of work. Labour's approach was to target resources on the poorest. The Pension Credit offered more money to the poorest pensioners, subject to means-testing, which undoubtedly helped the poorest in the short term but was seen by critics as discouraging saving. Meanwhile, to encourage the poorest as work rather than live on benefits, the Working Families Tax Credit saw lower rates of tax charged to low-paid workers with families. This related to Labour's plan, announced in 1999, to abolish child poverty in twenty years. Labour made good progress towards this goal in the early years of its time in office, but as that drew to a close in the midst of a recession, one newspaper headline read 'Labour's record on poverty in tatters' as it seemed to be not even halfway towards its target after thirteen years in power.[21]

During 2010–15 the costs of social security came under increasing scrutiny as part of the government's plan to cut the budget deficit. The government protected overall levels of pensions and pensioner benefits, and the Liberal Democrat pensions minister, Steve Webb, led the introduction of a single state pension, set above the level of the means test, to replace the existing two-tier system of basic pension plus various add-ons, which was presented as a return to the basic principles of the Beveridge Report.[22] However, there were significant cuts to other areas of the social security budget with £15 billion saved over 2010–15, and further cuts of a similar size thereafter.[23]

Environment

Arguably the most important issue we now face is one which has until now attracted insufficient political attention, even if the membership of environmentally concerned groups has been steadily on the increase. It was not until the 1980s that there was any significant UK legislation dealing with environmental matters other than water, air and noise pollution. While important in its own right, such legislation did not even begin to deal with issues of resource use and whether our economic system was sustainable, even though the 1972 UN Conference on the Human Environment had raised such concerns.

The idea of 'sustainability' first gained major global attention in 1987 through *Our Common Future*, the report of the Brundtland Commission (in full, the World Commission on Environment and Development, established by the United

Nations in 1983). It argued that the world could not sustain its current economic growth and meet the needs of the whole population, arguing that there needed to be a new way of living which 'meets the needs of the present without compromising the ability of future generations to meet their own needs'.[24]

Around the time that the Brundtland report was published, the Conservatives took some important steps. Margaret Thatcher's speech on climate change and ozone depletion is mentioned later (see p. 176), but there were also practical moves. In 1989 a report commissioned by the Department of the Environment, *Blueprint for a Green Economy* (known as the *Pearce Report*) explored, for example, how the economics of a sustainable environment could play a part in government. The 1990 Environmental Protection Act put forward measures to implement the 'polluters pay' principle. A fuel duty 'escalator' was introduced to steadily make fuel for motor vehicles more expensive (in the hope that this would discourage their use). Four 1994 documents[25] set out a range of policy proposals, although they were criticised for being timid on specific targets. Meanwhile, in 1995, the Environment Agency was established with a wide range of powers.

On the crucial issue of climate change, Labour pledged in 1997 that it would go further than the Conservatives. It set a target in its manifesto of reducing carbon dioxide emissions to twenty percent below 1990 levels, and so willingly signed up to the international Kyoto Protocol through which the UK agreed a cut of just 12.5% on 1990 figures by 2010. Labour met the Kyoto target but, due to rapid increases in energy demand as people drove bigger cars and used ever more gadgets, missed its self-set goal. Moreover, across Europe (including the UK), once the consumption of goods produced outside the EU was factored in, it was argued that, far from reducing emissions, European countries were actually increasing them.[26]

Labour's record elsewhere on the environment was mixed. In the face of public protests over fuel prices in 2000 it actually dropped the price escalator introduced by the Conservatives. Its attempts to place the environment at the heart of policy-making have been mixed, with environmental responsibilities regularly shifted around different departments as part of successive Cabinet reshuffles. When John Prescott, as Secretary of State for the Environment, Transport and the Regions was found to have access to two Jaguar cars, it seemed to symbolise Labour's ambivalent attitude to the environment – even if car use rather than car ownership is the most important issue to tackle. Other measures set out long-term strategies, particularly the Climate Change Act of 2008, which put forward new targets to reduce carbon dioxide emissions by eighty percent by 2050 compared to 1990 levels, and twenty-six percent by 2020. However, it remains to be seen how this will be achieved without significant extra investment in renewable energy sources such as wind power.

In opposition, David Cameron made much of how the Conservative Party was committed to tackling environmental problems, although this became less of a campaign priority when the recession started to bite. For the coalition, there was an immediate conflict over energy policy, because the Conservatives were for nuclear power and the Liberal Democrats against. It was the latter party which was given the energy and climate change portfolio in government. In 2015, Liberal Democrats claimed that policies such as increased investment in renewable energy, the establishment of the Green Investment Bank and the introduction of charges for plastic bags made the coalition 'the greenest government ever'. Critics pointed to the government's record on targets and fracking, and the extent to which, rhetorically, the Conservatives seemed to have ceased to give any priority to the green agenda.[27]

7

Power without responsibility: the media

The relationship between politics and the media is complex. To some extent they depend on each other. Politicians need the media to report what they do. The media needs the politician for a story. Yet the relationship has been a tense one for as long as both trades have existed. For politicians, the media all too often simplifies complex issues, reports froth and scandal, and gives the public a simplistic view of what politicians are like, all just to sell newspapers. Stanley Baldwin described two of the press barons of the inter-war years as exercising 'power without responsibility, the prerogative of the harlot throughout the ages'[1] and that view persists among modern politicians. For many journalists, politicians are there to be exposed, so that the public can find out what they are really up to. In so doing, journalists try to take the moral high ground by wielding a 'sword of truth'. Politicians try to do the same by saying that at least they are elected.

What is the media?

Defining what the media is was once very simple: forms of the printed word that carried news and/or comment on recent events, essentially newspapers, but also other periodical publications whether weeklies or monthlies. Once newspapers emerged to replace word of mouth, until the advent of radio in the 1920s, people got their news largely from newspapers. Despite persistent talk of the decline of the printed word, newspapers still remain remarkably popular as a way for people to access not only news, but opinion about news. However, since the 1920s for radio, and the 1950s for television, the 'broadcast media' has been just as important as a source of news because of its immediacy and visual power. Since the development of satellite and cable TV in the mid-1990s, and the more recent wide availability of digital channels without a subscription, the 'rolling' twenty-four-hour news offered by channels such as BBC News (formerly News 24) and Sky News has changed the way people access information. It has also changed the way in which politicians respond to news because there is a constant demand for new information to feed the appetites of news channels and their viewers. Stories which once took days to unfold now develop in hours as TV cameras are planted on the doorstep of any politicians involved in a dispute, crisis or scandal, and their utterances can be reported in minutes rather than awaiting a nightly news bulletin.

Although newspapers and the broadcast media still dominate news provision, electronic media of various types are revolutionising the way in which people find out about politics. For a start, the traditional newspaper and broadcast providers are increasingly putting material online and usually making it freely available. So although people still like to buy daily newspapers, they can often access the entire content of them online. This is one reason why newspapers resort to freebies such as CDs, DVDs, posters and a range of other collectable items in an attempt to persuade people to buy their product. Ultimately, the internet does pose a threat to the revenue of newspapers and we may soon reach a point where paying for online content becomes the norm rather than the exception. The figures certainly provide much for newspaper proprietors to worry about. At the end of 2001, the *Sun* had a circulation of 3.3 million, the *Mail* of over 2.3 million, and the *Guardian* over 380,000. By July 2015, the *Guardian*'s average daily circulation was down to 166,369, the *Sun* to 1,856,790 and the *Mail* to 1,627,706.[2]

Social media may not be 'media' in the traditional sense because they allow politicians to communicate directly with the public without having their message 'mediated' (that is, interpreted) by a journalist. This category of new media includes the plethora of websites, blogs, social networking platforms such as Facebook and Twitter, and broadcast channels such as YouTube. One of the earlier uses of video blogs was David Cameron's 'Webcameron', while bloggers such as Iain Dale, 'Guido Fawkes' and James Graham, have played important roles in debates in parties or more widely.[3] By 2010, almost all parliamentary candidates had a website and possibly a Facebook page, with some using Twitter. By 2015, these were requirements for all, with Twitter in particular helping politicians reach large numbers of people directly.[4] Politicians rightly spend time on social media because while many people still prefer to get their news from a provider they trust to be neutral, an increasing section of the population, especially younger people, head first to social media.

TWITTER – UPS AND DOWNS

Twitter is used by politicians to bypass the traditional media and communicate directly with the public. By far the most active party on Twitter is Labour,[5] but that fact alone suggests that activity on Twitter does not necessarily translate to general election success. Undoubtedly, Twitter has helped politicians achieve the connection they seek. However, it does not always work in their favour. In March 2014, David Cameron was widely mocked when his Twitter feed included a picture of him looking serious while talking to

TWITTER – UPS AND DOWNS (cont.)

Barack Obama on the telephone. In April 2011, Ed Balls accidentally tweeted his own name, only to be retweeted over 50,000 times. In June 2013, George Osborne landed himself in difficulties over a picture of him eating a 'posh' burger. A misspelling caused problems for Ed Miliband when paying tribute to TV personality Bob Holness in January 2012.[6]

How do the media and politics interact?

The relationships between politicians, the media and the public are complicated. It is generally agreed that there are at least five different categories of media influence:[7] reinforcement, manipulation, agenda-setting, priming/framing and direct.

The most overt form of influence is direct, where the media has a very specific impact on the issues people think about and the way they think about them. Often, direct influence is considered to be that where the public would not even be aware of an issue without the media bringing it to their attention. This can partly be about awareness-raising: if a newspaper or broadcaster pays attention to an issue then people become more aware of it and may decide to do something about it. In 1984, BBC reporter Michael Buerk reported from Ethiopia on 'a biblical famine ... the closest thing to hell on earth'. Watching the broadcast was the rock musician Bob Geldof, who was directly inspired to launch the Live Aid campaign which raised millions to help tackle the famine.[8] It was a truly harrowing broadcast, but one which helped inspire action to save lives.

Other 'direct' influence may be, as Michael Moran has argued, quite 'marginal' in its scope but may have 'critical' effects which decisively influence major events.[9] He points to the way many post-war elections are decided by a relatively small number of seats, with those seats being won by a relatively small number of votes. The most overt example of this is the *Sun*'s treatment of Neil Kinnock during the 1992 election. He was ridiculed throughout the campaign and on polling day itself the newspaper's front page carried a picture of Kinnock's head in a light bulb, with a headline 'If Kinnock wins today will the last person to leave Britain please turn out the lights.'[10] This coverage was typical, and rarely did the media say anything positive about Kinnock. It could only have a direct and negative impact on the public's view of Kinnock as a potential Prime Minister. The media came close to this in 2010 with some newspapers' treatment of Nick Clegg. Several slurs with tenuous foundations were made after the rightwing media became alarmed about his performance in the first leaders' debate of the campaign. Initially, these attacks were held to have backfired as there was no immediate dip in support for Clegg's party. However, there may have been an impact on the eventual election result with the Liberal Democrats gaining fewer votes than the opinion polls had predicted. Exactly the same applied to Ed Miliband and Labour in 2015.

A more far-reaching view of how the media affects opinion is through direct manipulation of politicians through the power of the press. For example, it is widely said that during Blair's time as Prime Minister, he was conscious on a daily basis of the influence of the newspapers owned by Rupert Murdoch through News International. The editorial line of the newspapers in this group was set against British membership of the Euro and Blair was said to have felt that while that remained the case, there was nothing he could do to take Britain into a single currency.

In more subtle ways, the media is seen to have an effect by reinforcing views. This particularly applies to the newspapers because, when buying one, people tend to know that newspapers have a political tendency and they generally buy one that matches their own views. Indeed, many people will only buy newspapers which give them what they want and so arguably it is not the newspapers that are leading the public, but the public who are defining what different newspapers must say if they want to survive in a competitive market. People who think along the lines of 'there is too much poverty and it could be dealt with if some people weren't so selfish' will find plenty of columnists who take a similar view in the *Guardian*. Moreover, they will find news stories that provide the evidence to support such a view. Meanwhile, somebody who feels that 'the country is in decline and the liberal establishment is undermining the moral standards of the young' will find the *Daily Mail* contains plenty to support such a view, from columnists, from the type of news that is reported, and the 'shock horror' style in which such news is presented. In these ways, existing views are reinforced, but it can also happen in more subtle ways through subconscious (or even conscious) editing by news consumers of less overtly biased sources. For example, somebody who is bothered about the issue of teenage pregnancies might pay far more attention to a BBC News item on the subject and draw from it those points which best support his/her existing view. In the same bulletin there might be stories about poverty or education, both of which are connected to teenage pregnancy, but they may be completely overlooked by somebody who looks at the issue from a particular perspective and therefore doesn't see a link.

Subtle control can also be exerted through the setting of agendas by the media. To some extent this is related to direct impact, as in the case of the broadcast from Ethiopia, but it is less dramatic. With agenda-setting, the media doesn't precisely control what people think, but it does affect what people think about. For example, in the summer of 2008, there was a spate of stories about knife crime among young people, especially in London. This put the issue on the political agenda because people became concerned about it having seen it in the media. Knife crime is not a new issue, nor has it gone away since 2008.

However, its current lack of prominence in the political agenda is nothing to do with the merits of the issue. Rather, the media is talking about it less than it briefly was when it judged the issue to be 'news'. As a result, politicians are asked about it less frequently and so they pay less attention to it.

Finally, and also related to agenda-setting, is 'priming/framing'. Both are ways of looking at how the media presents a story, and how that affects responses. For example, at election time, does the media focus on issues or party leaders? It may well be the case that one party has policies which are more in tune with the national mood, but another has a generally more popular leader. A focus more on policy or more on personalities could have an impact on how people vote. Alternatively, the media might focus attention on issues on which one party is stronger than another. For much of the post-war period, Labour has been seen as strongest on health policy, so if the media is concerned about that issue above others, and voters therefore think about it more, then Labour is likely to be the beneficiary.

Examples of priming/framing can be seen in the leaders' debates during the 2010 and 2015 elections. For much of the run-up to the 2010 election the media had persisted in talking about 'the two main parties' and had used phrases such as 'whichever of the two main parties is in government'. This encouraged people to perceive politics in a particular way. However, with three party leaders suddenly given equal billing perceptions changed and voters gave serious thought to the Liberal Democrats when they had not done so previously. Then, in 2015, the broadening of the menu of choices was even more marked with the leaders of the SNP, Plaid Cymru, UKIP and the Greens taking part in these televised debates.

We can see other practical effects of some of the issues highlighted above by comparing the way in which newspapers report big events. Each year, in March or April, the Chancellor of the Exchequer announces the government's

Budget, setting out spending plans for the year ahead. In 2005 the budget had particular political significance because it was close to a general election and could be seen in the context of the country being about to vote. Examining the front pages of the main national newspapers points towards a number of features of the way in which the same event was reported in quite different ways.

We see that first in the headlines. Three of the newspapers (*The Times*, the *Telegraph* and the *Independent*) took the same overall message from the Budget: their headlines focused on Gordon Brown's plans to give more to pensioners. Two other newspapers, the *Financial Times* and the *Guardian*, focused on a wider package of measures which would give money to different groups of people.

More emotive headlines in four newspapers took a different approach. The Conservatives had criticised the Budget for being about giveaways now, with the cost deferred until after the election. This was all reflected in critical headlines such as 'It's the rob you later budget' (the *Express*), 'Beware the bribes of March!' (the *Sun*) and 'You can pay me back later!' (the *Mail*). The *Daily Star* was the only major national paper not to lead on the Budget on the front page. In its judgement, what would most interest its potential readers was a story headed 'Gay secret of axe murder' alongside an entirely unrelated photograph of a woman wearing few clothes. However, inside the newspaper the Budget coverage carried a headline, 'Here comes the bribe'. Only one newspaper, the Labour-supporting *Mirror*, carried a story that was as positive as the other tabloids were negative. It pictured Gordon Brown as the Disney character Mr Incredible. The headline simply read 'Mr Incredible' with a number of the policies picked out in bubbles.

The most overt differences between the papers can be seen in the front-page headlines. The critical headlines in the *Express*, *Mail* and *Sun* reflected an editorial line at the time that was generally anti-Labour and increasingly pro-Conservative. They had essentially replayed the critique of the Budget offered by the Conservatives. Where a newspaper was inclined towards the Conservatives but had not offered a critical headline, as in the case of the *Telegraph*, the editors had a made a judgement about the style of journalism their readers liked and had concluded that the 'wham bam' type of headline used by tabloids was not appropriate for *Telegraph* readers. But one only has to scratch a little below the headline to find the editorial line picked out in a text box: the newspaper said of Gordon Brown, 'He is like a mugger who says he will hit you six times but who then announces that, after further consideration, he will only hit you five times instead.' They also replayed Michael Howard's 'vote now, pay later' critique.

More subtle, but nonetheless interesting, is the choice made by editors over which specific details of the Budget to highlight in summaries which appeared on many of the front pages. We can see this most clearly by comparing two Labour-aligned newspapers. The *Guardian* led on the £200 council tax rebate for pensioners, and changes to stamp duty and inheritance tax. The *Mirror* also included the council tax change, but went further on pensioners and referred to 'free bus fares for OAPs'. Meanwhile, aside from mentioning extra money for schools and colleges, it picked increases to child benefits and tax credits, and flagged more childcare provision. In these cases we can see the judgement of the respective editors about the interests of their readers (or potential readers). The wealthier *Guardian* readers are seen to be more interested in stamp duty (because they are more likely to be home buyers) and inheritance tax (because they are more likely to be involved in leaving or inheriting large assets). Meanwhile, *Mirror* readers are more likely to be on low incomes (and so be affected by tax credits) or be poorer pensioners (and so find free bus fares more interesting than inheritance tax).

How biased is the media?

So in light of all this, just how biased is the media? Some problems of bias and/or inaccuracy arise from practical problems. Most journalists operate under very tight deadlines and everyone understands that getting it right quickly can be difficult. Moreover, the media has to summarise, interpret and investigate. In performing these roles, some people are bound to be unhappy about what the media does and to see the results as biased.

On the surface, there are very clear safeguards against some bias and overdominance of the market. There are also complaints procedures for when the media makes mistakes so that amends can be made. The Monopolies and Mergers Commission has the power to rule against agglomerations of ownership which threaten to put too much media in control of one individual or a group. The Press Complaints Commission can adjudicate when people feel they have been treated unfairly or wrongly by the press. OFCOM (Office of Communications) performs a similar role for broadcast media. As regards television, commercial TV is obliged by law to be neutral and balanced in the way it handles election campaigns, and the BBC behaves in the same way voluntarily. But that doesn't apply outside election time and imbalances can occur.

Compared to television and radio, newspapers are much more free to do and say what they like, so long as they are not libellous. This is where the political views of editors and owners can have a real effect, and it is often with the newspapers that the politician becomes most frustrated.

Many politicians certainly believe that the media now has an increasingly negative impact on public life. Soon after he left office, Tony Blair said in a major speech:

> I do believe this relationship between public life and media is now damaged in a manner that requires repair. The damage saps the country's confidence and self-belief; it undermines its assess-

ment of itself, its institutions; and above all, it reduces our capacity to take the right decisions, in the right spirit for our future.[11]

Blair also argued, 'It is sometimes said that the media is accountable daily through the choice of readers and viewers. That is true up to a point. But the reality is that the viewers or readers have no objective yardstick to measure what they are being told.'

Perhaps Blair's comments were partly the natural conclusion reached by someone who had been hammered by the press on a number of issues. But most people who have been involved in politics, even strong opponents of Blair, will feel some sympathy with what he said. My own experience of working in politics is that I came across some really excellent journalists, who were genuinely interested in getting to the heart of the matter. But they operated in a system where personalities were often more interesting than policy issues, and so-called 'news' (that is, what is new) was pursued at the expense of what was consistent. Moreover, journalists who are based at Westminster inhabit a world that is even more unreal than the world in which politicians live. Unlike Westminster politicians, journalists don't have to face the public to be elected, they don't have to deal with local casework, and they don't go out knocking on doors on housing estates in the wind and the rain. They are also, often, very highly paid and quite out of touch with how people live their day-to-day lives. That was brought home to me when trying to explain to two otherwise excellent journalists about the former Liberal Democrat policy of charging a tax rate of fifty percent on earnings over £100,000 per year. At the time, such earnings were enjoyed by only one percent of taxpayers yet it was put to me that such a policy would hit 'middle income' people. Clearly, these journalists had no idea that 'middle income' actually meant around £22,000 per year at the time, and it was frustrating to know that such people have such power over what the ordinary public gets to know about politicians.

This can lead to a very distorted view by the public of what politicians are proposing.

However, there are many journalists who have argued that the blame for these problems lies on both sides of the media/politics divide. Both Jeremy Paxman and Nick Robinson have made thoughtful contributions to the debate in public lectures.[12] Robinson summed up the difficult relationship between the media and politicians when he said: 'Divorce is not an option. Neither is easy contentment. We are doomed to live together. Let's work at it and stop whingeing each about the other.' Paxman argued that there was more common ground between journalists and politicians than many allow, and was critical of the way in which the media reacted to Blair's speech about the media:

> I thought the way we responded to Tony Blair's speech was pretty pathetic ... These two trades, politics and media, have a great deal in common. Both deal in words and images, both involve a contract with the public based upon fairly explicit promises. And both are trades best practised by people who aren't over-encumbered with a sense of their own frailty. We are also, of course, both down there with estate agents and car dealers when it comes to public affection and trust. Look at the charts: producers do rank just above paedophiles. Just.

Though he had plenty of criticisms to make of Blair, Paxman went on to say:

> The basic charge sheet against us from Tony Blair and Alastair Campbell is as follows. Firstly, that we behave like a herd. Secondly, that we have a trivial and collective judgement. Thirdly, that we prefer sensation to understanding. I'm sorry to say, but I think there's something in all of these arguments.

Criticism of the media has come from some other unlikely sources. Former BBC political editor Andrew Marr is an example of the cult of the commentator who can dominate a story above the policy content or the politicians. Despite that, he has raised some serious concerns about the media and how it treats politicians. In his book on journalism, he describes the broad news agenda as telling an 'overarching story about public life' in which 'everyone in it is a lying hypocrite who deserves ridicule; which downgrades any thought that public life can include genuine idealism, some self-sacrifice, hard work and interesting thinking'. He goes on to say, 'political journalists have spent too much time metaphorically jamming wastebins on politicians' heads. We have become too powerful, too much the interpreters, using our talents as communicators to crowd them out.'[13] Is it any wonder that politicians feel defensive about the media?

How politicians deal with the media: spin

One word dominates the way the public sees politicians as dealing with the media: spin. This word has, in recent decades, been used to describe the efforts of politicians to get across their message. It is widely condemned for being a deceptive 'dark act' yet it is not nearly as mysterious as people imagine. It has been driven by politicians thinking about how they can overcome media bias and also feed the demand. As Tony Blair said, 'a vast aspect of our jobs today – outside of the really major decisions, as big as anything else – is coping with the media, its sheer scale, weight and constant hyperactivity.'[14]

On an individual level, the ultimate aim of any politicians in dealing with the media is to get themselves and their message portrayed in a positive light. This is ultimately all that spin amounts to. They do it in a number of ways which are actually quite similar to how people operate in a range of activities in day-to-day life, and we should not be surprised about that.

Fundamentally, politicians build relationships with people who can help them to get their message across. Very few journalists will cover any story from a politician they have never heard of, unless it's the kind of news story that has news value in its own right – often because it involves some kind of scandal and/or corruption.

So it is in a politician's interest to be known to journalists on a one-to-one basis. That does not mean knowing them as friends, although that does happen, but it does mean knowing them professionally. In short, politicians do what people do in all sorts of spheres of daily life: they network. Alternatively, politicians can approach journalists using people who are already known by the journalist, which is where professional press officers come in, especially those employed by political parties. It should be said that these relationships are not always one-way, in fact far from it: any up-and-coming journalist wants to get to know the movers and shakers of politics because, for reasons discussed later, this can open up new sources of stories which in turn can help to make a journalist's reputation for being at the cutting edge of his/her trade.

Whether going directly to a journalist or through a press officer, there are some very straightforward tools of the trade which can help a politician get a story into the media. When I worked for a new think tank in Westminster in 1998, and we were launching our first publications, I naively assumed that all we had to do to get publicity was send out a press release advertising press conferences at which people would make earnest statements about the publications in question. I assumed that journalists would just turn up and listen to what we had to say. That's surely what they do all day long, isn't it? Wrong. A friendly press officer in another organisation pointed out that journalists receive many more press releases in a day than they can ever read, and they have very little time to turn up to press conferences. Instead, he advised not doing a general release and instead offering the publication to a carefully selected journalist (from a newspaper with readers interested in the subject) on an 'exclusive' basis. That's what we did, and it basically worked, and that is at the core of what politicians do with many of their stories. Journalists are willing to do it because 'exclusive' means that nobody else has the story and anyone interested in it has to buy their product if they want that story. In time, if they get enough similar stories, it can help people come to the conclusion that they need to buy that newspaper more often to read the kinds of stories, they like. For politicians, the exclusive story has an advantage because it can get them coverage they might not otherwise get. Moreover, it can get them coverage in a carefully selected newspaper when they actively wouldn't want coverage elsewhere. For example, a politician taking a 'tough' stance on immigration might want coverage in the *Mail* but not in the *Independent*, simply because such a position is likely to enthuse *Mail* readers but put off those who read the *Independent*.

Such targeted coverage is also an advantage of the advance story, where an item is going to be on general release, but one or more newspapers or broadcasters is given an early peek at what the document contains. For example, in between elections, political parties often publish summaries of their overall values and policies. These are sometimes called pre-manifestos because they are published in advance of the main general election manifesto. Any party is going to have some messages which appeal to some audiences more than others and, in advance of the formal launch of such a document, different parts of it can be given to different newspapers in order to try to get them to cover it in the most favourable way possible. Of course, any journalists worth their wages will try to find out more about the document than the party initially wants to give them, and they will often be successful in doing that. However, the party usually gets to direct the coverage in a particular way. While this may sound underhand, there is no objective reason why the politician's view of what should be covered is of less value than the preoccupations of the newspapers' editors. If newspapers persist in writing about their concerns, they must expect politicians to push their concerns at the same time. It's all part of the same transaction and both sides understand the unwritten rules well enough.

Of course, there are occasions on which parties and politicians don't give any advance insights into a document or statement and just launch it to everyone. General election manifestos are a case in point, because almost all media outlets try to cover the main manifestos in the same depth and accept that the launch of a manifesto is newsworthy in its own right. In fact, doing anything other than launching it to all at the same time can actually undermine coverage because it reduces the extent to which the manifesto contents are news to anybody. In such a situation, public release to all at the same time often suits everyone.

Aside from launches of new statements or initiatives, politicians also seek to influence the news in a number of less overt ways. Journalists are very willing to take politicians out to lunch if they think they can get a story out of it, or if they think they can learn useful background information that will help them to do their job in a way that is better informed. Remember that lunch at swanky restaurants can be claimed by journalists on expenses, but not by politicians, despite the high and mighty tone of many journalists on the subject: the arrangement suits both sides. Such occasions are a crucial part of the development of a close professional relationship between politician and journalist and can lead to a situation where journalists have 'inside' sources of information. They are not usually, and should not be, about exchanging 'secrets', but they can lead to better understanding of what goes on inside a party on the part of the journalist. From the politician's perspective, ensuring that journalists are well informed so that they can write intelligently about a subject of mutual interest has a value in itself. Meanwhile, the politician might even get to place a story.

Underpinning all of these methods for getting across their point, political parties have highly thought-through media strategies. At the core of any such strategy is a political 'message'. This is simply what people learn from an exposure to politicians, although it may have unintended consequences. More often than not, politicians have overarching messages which they do a number of things to reinforce. In recent times, the Labour Party has been most adept at doing that. For example, when Neil Kinnock became leader of the Labour Party in 1983 he wanted to get across to the public the idea that Labour was no longer the hard-left party it had appeared to be at the previous election. He changed policy in a number of key areas to give such claims substance. He reduced the influence of trades unions on selection of parliamentary candidates to try to reduce left-wing influence on MPs. He had a public row with the leaders of Militant, the Trotskyite faction within the Labour Party. Contentious debates at party conferences were replaced by set-piece speeches from well-known national figures. The party logo was changed from a red flag to a red rose. All of these changes, some of substance and some of symbolism, were linked to an overall message that people could trust Labour to govern the country, and they were continued by both John Smith and Tony Blair. When Labour was elected in 1997, it was the triumph of the most effective political rebranding ever in British politics.

Other messaging can have a more specific focus. In the run-up to the 1992 general election, the Liberal Democrats sought a distinctive policy to communicate their belief that public services were being underfunded by the Conservatives. The policy they developed for their 1992 manifesto, raising extra money for education by adding 1p to the basic rate of income tax, was a brave move because it came at a time when putting

up taxes ran against the orthodoxy of the day. Yet in proposing such a policy, the party communicated two things. First, it
got across the message that the party was serious about tackling
underfunding in education. Second, it suggested that the party
was willing to tell the truth about the choices facing the country,
even at the risk of electoral unpopularity. In fact, the policy was
extremely popular and served the party well in 1992 and two
subsequent general elections.

Of course, messages can backfire. The Liberal Democrat 1p
policy was seen by some as being a 'high tax' policy, but there
are better examples of a message going wrong. William Hague
made a number of mistakes in his time as Conservative leader.
When he attended the 1997 Notting Hill Carnival it was an
attempt to show the Conservatives in a different, multicultural
light. He was also meant to look youthful, as on the occasion
when he wore a baseball cap on a day out at Alton Towers.
He did look young, but a young nerd, deeply uncomfortable
on both occasions. Similarly, when David Cameron visited
Norway and was photographed with husky dogs, the aim was
to show him as a leader who was concerned about climate
change. Some of that was achieved, but many journalists asked
why they had been flown all the way to Norway for a photo
opportunity, despite all the environmental damage such a trip
would cause.

So this is spin. In its essential aspects it is little different to the
way many people communicate in many aspects of daily life. It
is largely an adaption to politics of communications techniques
used without criticism in many other walks of life. What has
changed in recent years is simply that politicians have got better
at it than they once were, and the media does not always like
that. But why should politicians not behave as the rest of the
country does when trying to get their message across? Let he
who is without spin cast the first stone.

Satire: the media and public's revenge?

Whatever politicians try to do to get their message across, there is one form of media on which they can have very little effect: satire. This is not new in politics. The political cartoon has been around for centuries. The eighteenth century saw especially savage treatments of the politicians of the day. In recent times, cartoonists have had the ability to shape views of politicians in a way that can have a fatal impact on people's careers. The *Guardian* cartoonist Steve Bell famously pictured John Major as a man who was so incompetent that he put his underpants on over his trousers. The same cartoonist also did great damage to Menzies Campbell (Liberal Democrat leader in 2006-7) by picturing him as a very elderly man who needed to walk using a zimmer frame, even though he was only in his early sixties.

A more recent phenomenon has been the rise of television satire. Until the 1960s, broadcasters were very reluctant to show anything negative about politicians. Indeed, in general journalists took quite a deferential approach to interviewing them. On one occasion during the 1951 general election campaign, Clement Attlee was asked a series of very soft questions, including 'Anything else you would care to say about the coming election?' to which he replied 'No' and the matter was left at that.[15] No journalist would now let a politician get away with that and there are even clearer signs of the loss of respect for politicians in the rise of satire.

In the 1950s there was mild mockery of politicians in *The Goon Show* on radio, with Peter Sellers playing Winston Churchill, but the humour was gentle. That changed in 1962 with the launch of *That Was The Week That Was* (known for short as *TW3*), fronted by David Frost with many of the leading comedians of the day appearing. Its treatment of politicians was merciless, so much so that it only ran for two years because the

BBC was worried that it would pose problems if it ran in the election year of 1964. But even though it was cancelled, it had opened the possibility of political satire on television and since then this has been a major part of the public's engagement with politics. From 1984 to 1996, *Spitting Image* played a crucial role in influencing public views of the Cabinet, for example, with Margaret Thatcher as a domineering figure, Norman Tebbit as her hard-man boot boy and Kenneth Baker as a slimy snail. The images had an effect because they related to what people already felt about the politicians concerned, but by being so vivid they actually helped to create some images.

There is nothing quite like *Spitting Image* today, but other shows aired more recently, such as *The Thick of It* and *Bremner, Bird and Fortune*, have been important ways in which fun has been poked at politicians in public. What is particularly interesting about the role of politics in the entertainment industry in the UK is that the top political shows are satire, and often savage satire at that. We have nothing like the optimistic and inspirational American hit drama *The West Wing*. That tells us a lot about quite how cynical the British public is about politics. If spin is the way that politicians deal with the media and the voters, satire offers the public a little revenge.

The future

The relationship between the media and politics is certainly in crisis. For all the informed comment on the relationship between the two, the overwhelming atmosphere is still one of tension. It is difficult to know how this can change easily or quickly. Journalists will still try to find out what politicians aren't telling you – it's part of their job. Politicians will still try to get their message across in the best way they can, in the best possible light – it's part of their job – and with so many people out there ready to scrutinise what they do, who can blame them for putting forward as much positive spin as possible?

This is why so many politicians find social media an appealing way of directly communicating with the public. Of course, they will still have to bother about what the newspaper and TV commentators say, because these people have the ability to influence the public mood. But with it becoming easier than ever before for politicians to access individual voters through social media, we can expect to see more and more of such campaigning in future.

8

Losing an Empire, finding a role: British politics and the wider world

In 1945, Britain ruled twenty-five percent of the world's population. Now, it has responsibility for little more outside the UK than Gibraltar, the Falkland Islands and some small territories in the Pacific and Caribbean. At the same time, the British economy has fallen behind many competitors in relative terms. Yet whenever there is a major military operation to be launched (for example, in Kosovo, Afghanistan or Iraq), the UK still behaves like a major power. Much of Britain's remaining world power seems to rest on clinging to a 'special relationship' with the USA which, in the Obama era, the USA seems far less interested in than it was under Presidents Clinton or Bush.

Decline and declinism

One of the dominant features of post-war British politics has been a sense that Britain is a nation in decline: dominating many political debates is a sense that we used to lead the world in many areas, but now do it in almost none. It's a theme which has led some writers to talk about 'declinism' as a state of mind.[1] As Geoffrey Howe said, in his first Budget speech in 1979, 'In the last few years the hard facts of our relative decline have become increasingly plain, and the threat of absolute decline has gradually become very real.'[2] This is actually not as new a complaint as we sometimes imagine. In 1777, Adam Smith's *Wealth of Nations* pointed out that there were regular complaints that 'the wealth of the nation was fast declining'.[3] A century on, in 1902, when the British Empire was nearing its peak, Joseph Chamberlain saw the Empire as fundamentally weak, saying 'The weary Titan staggers under the too vast orb of its fate.'[4] Despite the British reputation for not grumbling (or at least trying not to), this has been a pretty constant refrain.

So it is in some ways remarkable that only eight years after Geoffrey Howe's complaint, the Conservative general election manifesto argued that the party had stopped British decline. Harking back to how it had entered office in 1979, it said:

> Remember the conventional wisdom of the day. The British people were 'ungovernable'. We were in the grip of an incurable 'British disease'. Britain was heading for 'irreversible decline'.
>
> Well the people were *not* ungovernable, the disease was *not* incurable, the decline *has* been reversed.[5]

How accurate a version of events is this view of Britain being in 'decline' in the post-war period? And has that really been turned round since the 1970s?

Since 1945, the British economy has grown according to all conventional measures, but so too has just about every economy in the world. Britain has not grown as fast as many, so what is being talked about above is relative decline. People have more money than ever before and they use that to obtain the trappings of materialism. Many will question the value of such 'progress', especially in terms of its environmental impact, but the basic truth is that, where we once measured poverty by whether or not children wore shoes, we now see it in terms of what sorts of electronic goods people have in their homes. But relative to the rest of the world, the UK has declined over the period as a whole, but with some improvements in relative growth since the 1970s. For example, compared to fifteen other western European countries, the UK's growth was ranked sixteenth (bottom) between 1950 and 1973, but rose slightly to joint twelfth in 1973–92. More recently, on average between 2001 and 2007, the UK had above average annual growth per year when compared to other OECD (Organisation for Economic Cooperation and Development) countries, although it was later hit more than most by the credit crunch because its economy was so reliant on debt.[6] However, where absolute decline has been clear is in Britain's place in the world as a great power.

Losing an Empire

Prior to 1945 there had been many measures of gradual independence for Britain's colonies. By 1945, countries such as Australia, New Zealand and Canada had been ruling themselves for many years. However, after the war, the way in which Britain lost the remainder of its Empire in little more than twenty years is a remarkable story. How was it that a country whose empire covered, at its peak, nearly one-quarter of the world's land and population, gave away control without much apparent regret?

Part of the answer to this question is found in the concept of Empire held by many of those who ran it. At the core of their belief in Empire was the idea of trusteeship.[7] The argument ran something like this. *Although there are economic and strategic benefits for Britain in holding colonies, it is not Britain's wish to impose rule on peoples who are capable of running their own government. When native peoples demonstrate that they can run their countries in a civilised way then they will be allowed to do so.* Of course, underpinning this idea were deeply patronising and essentially racist notions of what being 'civilised' entailed. In the view of many imperialists, there were some native peoples who would never be able to attain civilisation. However, the concept of trusteeship contained within it the seeds of destruction of the Empire. If the colonised were constantly told that they could rule themselves when they attained 'civilisation', then it was hard to resist that when they seemed to meet the criteria. In India, that became the case very clearly during the inter-war years. For example, one of the leaders of the Indian independence movement, and India's first Prime Minister, was Jawaharlal Nehru. He came from a wealthy family and was sent to England to be educated at Harrow School and Cambridge University. This gave him the same educational background as much of the British ruling class. It was hard to resist Nehru's claims to be able to rule his people in just the same way as those with a similar background ruled the UK.

However, the end of Empire was not solely about the nature of British imperialism. The role of colonial nationalist movements was crucial in persuading the British that it was time to leave, sometimes in the face of violence against the symbols and facts of British rule. Such activism often preceded a decision to leave. For example, the violent actions of groups who wanted an Israeli state led to British withdrawal from Palestine in 1947, and the activities of the 'Mau Mau' in Kenya were the first sign of the costs of remaining, unwelcome, in African colonies.

There were also pressures on Britain to surrender its imperial role because it became increasingly apparent that it no longer matched Britain's power on the world stage. That became very clear in 1956 during the Suez crisis. This saw Britain and France collaborating in an attempt to take control of the Suez Canal, which was crucial to their global trading interests and which the Egyptian leader, Nasser, had nationalised. When British and French troops landed in the area the action was denounced by the Americans and both countries were forced to withdraw in the face of international condemnation. It was a triumph for

Nasser which inspired colonial independence movements to realise that Britain was weak and dependent on American support for much of its prestige in the world.

There is also a debate about how far the British Empire was undermined by the focus of post-war British politics on the development of the welfare state. Opinion is divided among academics but one thing is clear: there was no major public demand to maintain colonies that wanted independence. In contrast, the public did want high levels of spending on schools, hospitals and pensions, and had there been a competition over maintaining an Empire or funding these, public opinion would have been clear. At the same time, there was a general international political consensus that formal empires were no longer acceptable. In particular, American public and political opinion was inspired by

POST-WAR END OF BRITISH RULE

1946	Jordan
1947	India and Pakistan; Palestine handed over to United Nations
1948	Burma and Ceylon (Sri Lanka)
1956	Sudan
1957	Malaya and Ghana
1960	Nigeria and Cyprus
1961	Sierra Leone and Tanganyika (Tanzania)
1962	Jamaica, Trinidad and Uganda
1963	Kenya
1964	Malawi, Zambia and Malta
1965	Gambia, Rhodesia's Unilateral Declaration of Independence
1966	Guyana, Lesotho, Botswana and Barbados
1968	Mauritius and Swaziland
1970	Fiji
1973	Bahamas
1980	Zimbabwe (formerly Rhodesia) established as majority rule state
1997	Hong Kong

the USA's history of throwing off colonial rule. It saw mirror images of its own past in struggles against British dominion.

Finding a role

The former US Secretary of State Dean Acheson commented in 1962 that the UK had lost an Empire but not yet found a role. At the time he spoke, many British policy makers believed that they *had* found a role but had not yet brought it to fruition. That role was as a leader in Europe. There had been talk of some kind of European political union as far back as the 1920s and there had been a small body of opinion in the UK in favour, not only of there being a European federation, but of Britain being a part of it. However, Britain came out of the Second World War full of confidence about its power. While it was willing to encourage formal political cooperation between European countries, there was no significant argument in favour of British participation in anything like a political union. In the late 1940s the UK did sign treaties on defence (the 1947 Treaty of Dunkirk with France) and on financial, cultural and social cooperation (the 1948 Brussels Pact with Belgium, the Netherlands, Luxembourg and France). It also joined the Council of Europe in 1949, but that was merely a consultative body and the UK (along with the Scandinavian countries) firmly rejected anything approaching, for example, a customs union.

The British position was that it felt powerful in its own right, and was keen to have a close relationship with the USA. One of its priorities in the late 1940s was to secure American participation in the North Atlantic Treaty Organisation (NATO), which it did in 1949. The aim of NATO was to offer defence against the Soviet Union's military might, and British policy-makers were clear that it would only work if the USA took part. Meanwhile, Britain was heavily dependent on US financial support, through both a loan and Marshall aid. At this stage, the UK also had significant imperial commitments and while it was withdrawing from trouble spots such as India and Palestine it was not at all clear that other colonies would soon gain independence. Consequently, the British world view of the late 1940s and 1950s was summed up by Winston Churchill, who saw Britain's place in the world as being the only country which could interlock three circles of power: Empire, Europe and the USA. It did not want to lose that supposedly pivotal position by overcommitting to one at the expense of the others.

However, close political and economic cooperation was precisely what many European countries did want and they moved ahead without Britain. First, the Schuman Plan of May 1950 established joint control of the Franco–German coal and steel industries. The UK took no part. Then, in 1957, the Treaty of Rome established the European Economic Community. Initially with six members (France, West Germany, Italy, Belgium, the Netherlands and Luxembourg), it was both an area of free trade and a customs union.

FREE TRADE AREAS AND CUSTOMS UNIONS

- *Free trade area*: a group of countries that have agreed not to charge any tariffs on trade between each other. This is the loosest form of economic union.
- *Customs union*: a group of countries that have agreed to charge the same customs on trade with countries not in the union, in addition to trading without tariffs between each other.

The UK response to the formation of the EEC was sceptical, and few argued for British membership in 1957. However, the British government believed that there might be some benefits in joining a free trade area. So it negotiated the formation of one (the European Free Trade Association) in 1960 with Denmark, Sweden, Norway, Switzerland, Austria and Portugal. Even by the time the UK had joined EFTA it had been looking into EEC membership and negotiations began in 1961 under Harold Macmillan. The government had decided that it could benefit from membership both economically and politically, as it was growing ever more conscious that it was losing the influence which came with being a great imperial power. The negotiations came to nothing, however, partly because the French (probably rightly) feared that the UK would try to dominate the EEC. President de Gaulle therefore vetoed the application in 1963.

In the early 1960s, the Labour Party had been sceptical about British entry to the EEC. Many Labour members saw it as a capitalist club, but there were some pro-Europeans in the Labour ranks. Consequently, Labour made an application in 1967, but it was again vetoed by de Gaulle. For many in Edward Heath's generation of Conservatives, European unity was a passion. They believed that it would help to avoid the wars that had twice in living memory dragged Britain into a continental dispute. On his return to government in 1970, Heath pursued membership with vigour and, aided by de Gaulle no longer being President, successfully negotiated for British membership, to begin from 1 January 1973.

Labour was critical of some of the terms of entry to the EEC and pledged to try to get a better deal for the UK when it was next elected, and then to hold a referendum on whether to stay in or leave. This was largely a political device for Wilson to keep his party together because it was split on the issue. However, Wilson did manage to renegotiate some points, winning, for example, a rebate on some of the UK's contribution to the EEC budget, and the provision of funds for poorer parts of Europe through a regional development scheme. These measures enabled Wilson to tell the voters he had got a good deal for Britain, and to tell socialist critics in his own party that he had secured a progressive direction for the EEC. In the referendum held in 1975, which is to this day the only UK-wide referendum ever held, sixty-seven percent of those who voted wanted Britain to remain a member. They had been urged to vote this way by all the party leaders and most senior figures within all the main parties, and it was widely felt that this had settled Britain's place in Europe once and for all. As we saw earlier (pp. 63–4), this settled position saw European law have priority over that passed in the UK on any issue in which the EEC had authority.

Since the UK joined, Europe has been high on the political agenda for three main reasons, and at times all three factors have coincided. First, Labour and the Conservatives are both internally divided on Europe. That was particularly the case in the 1970s with Labour, and then in the 1990s among Conservatives. Neither party has shied away from using the issue of Europe as a form of public blood letting in which different groups try to wrest control of the party's direction. Second, there can be political value in appearing to be 'standing up' for Britain in Europe. Margaret Thatcher understood this very well and in her early years in office gained much political credit at home for being seen to negotiate hard on Britain's overall contribution to the EEC. Thatcher did this extremely effectively at the 1979 Dublin summit of leaders soon after she became Prime Minister and continued to do so annually until the 1984 Fontainebleu summit which appeared to resolve the issue in Britain's favour.

The third and most important factor in putting Europe on the political agenda is the drive in other European countries towards greater European unity. When British people voted in the 1975 referendum they were voting for membership of something that was exactly what its name suggested: an 'Economic Community'. However, since 1975 there has been a drive towards closer social and political cooperation, which has been extremely emotive in British politics. The major developments have come through new laws and treaties which have revised and expanded the role of Europe. In 1986, when Parliament passed the Single European Act, it was consenting to the creation of a full single market in 1992, and included, for example, provisions for standardising aspects of environment and employment law. Despite agreeing to this plan, Thatcher became increasingly concerned that 'Europe' brought with it the threat of greater state control and said in a speech in Bruges in 1988 that 'We have not successfully rolled back the frontiers of the state in Britain, only to see them reimposed at a European level, with a European super-state exercising a new dominance from Brussels.'[8]

This set the tone for a debate that divided Thatcher's party and ultimately led to her downfall. It also did nothing to prevent the UK signing up to the Maastricht Treaty of 1992 which established closer political union and collaboration. The treaty transformed the EEC into the European Union. In so doing, Maastricht set out the procedure which would lead to a single currency; established common European citizenship; brought justice, home affairs and foreign policy into the EU's realm; and laid down a framework for integrating social and employment legislation.

Subsequent treaties (Amsterdam in 1997, Nice in 2004 and Lisbon in 2007) have really only tweaked Maastricht, especially with a focus on how the EU's structures operate. Was Maastricht what Britain signed up for in 1973 or 1975? Certainly not, but it was agreed by the British government, voluntarily. When it came into force, Britain had completed its journey from Empire to European political union.

Wars in 'peacetime'

In seventy plus years of 'peace' since the end of the Second World War around 3,500 British servicemen and women have lost their lives in action. These losses came in eighteen separate conflicts and there has only been one year, 1968, in which there was not a death in action. Nearly half the losses came in just two of the conflicts: 765 in the Korean War of 1950–3 and 763 associated with the Troubles in Northern Ireland. Other conflicts in which there were high losses included the Malayan Emergency of 1948–60 (340 deaths), the Falklands War of 1982 (255) and the conflict in Palestine in 1945–8 (233). Most recently, the 2003–9 engagement in Iraq saw 179 British deaths, while losses in Afghanistan between 2001 and 2012 were 404.[9]

These losses might lead some to expect that involvement in wars has led to major political conflict in the UK but, in fact, there has been remarkably little controversy among politicians on issues relating to war. In part, that has been due to some reluctance among those who might oppose a war to be seen to be doing anything that undermines the work of British troops in combat. While troops are fighting abroad, almost all politicians are always keen to back them and to be seen to be doing so. That can have the effect of muting criticism of British policy as a whole and it did so most notably in the early stages of the 2003–9 intervention in Iraq. Prior to the war, the Liberal Democrats and many Labour politicians had voiced serious doubts about launching a strike on Saddam Hussein's regime, but once it had been done there was a resolve on all sides to do all they could to support British troops.

One conflict which might have been very controversial in Parliament had Britain been engaged in it was the Vietnam War. The USA was involved there throughout the 1960s and did not withdraw its troops until 1973. During this time, America wanted support from as many of its allies as possible and, in the mid to late 1960s, President Johnson was especially keen for Britain to become involved. As Prime Minister, Harold Wilson astutely resisted pressure from Johnson to commit even a token British force. Seeing the demonstrations on the streets against a war in which

Britain was not even involved was one factor which made it clear to Wilson that there would not be the usual domestic support for British troops if they became engaged in Vietnam. He had no desire to oppose public opinion on the issue.

There has only been one 'war' since 1945 which has caused a major row in Parliament and that was the Suez crisis of 1956. The British valued the Suez Canal for its importance as a trading route with the East, and when the Egyptian leader, Nasser, nationalised it, they felt that their interests were threatened. British military involvement in the Suez area followed a deal which the British and French had made secretly with Israel in August 1956. They agreed that if Israel attacked Egypt, then Britain and France would intervene, ostensibly as peacekeepers. That would involve separating Israeli and Egyptian forces and taking control of the canal apparently as neutral parties. The intervention in October and November 1956 saw the British and French engage Egyptian forces. The British lost twenty-two and the French fewer, but the Egyptians lost several hundred in addition to around 1,000 killed in the conflict with Israel.

Although the British–French operation was successful in seizing the canal, it was widely condemned, not least by the USA, which feared that the conflict could escalate with the Soviet Union supporting Egypt. Meanwhile, Prime Minister Eden came under attack in Parliament and more widely in public. The Labour leader, Hugh Gaitskell, made a radio broadcast criticising the way in which Britain had intervened without securing the agreement of the United Nations. Gaitskell referred to British 'obstruction' of the UN and added that Britain should only have gone into Suez as part of a UN force. He said, 'Make no mistake ... this is war' and said that Britain was 'opposed by the world, in defiance of the world' having 'taken the law into our own hands'.[10] The Liberal Party was also critical and there were public demonstrations. The government was so badly damaged that when Eden resigned in January 1957 it was clear that it was Suez which had done for him. By that point, British troops had already been forced to withdraw in the face of hostile world opinion.

There were parallels between Suez and the Iraq war of 2003–9, which did more than anything else to undermine Tony Blair and, ultimately, create the public mood which led to his resignation in 2007. Like Suez, this was a war in which countries engaged without the full authority of the United Nations. But even more so than Suez there was strong public opinion which said that war in Iraq would only be justified if it was in the name of the UN. Prior to the war, over one million people had demonstrated against it on the streets of London. Consequently, even though Blair secured a vote in Parliament (by 412 to 149 MPs) for British participation, initial public support fell away as soon as the war began to go badly. There was no shortage of people and politicians ready to say that they had warned against it.

Much anger over Iraq focused on Blair's relationship with President George W. Bush. From 1997, Blair had valued his close relationship with President Bill Clinton. There had even been something of a three-way relationship between Blair, Clinton and Chancellor Gerhard Schroeder of Germany. The three men not only had a similar view of world affairs and were willing to work together, but had also based their domestic electoral success on 'Third Way' ideas which embraced markets far more than was usual for centre-left politicians. When Bush became President in 2001, many expected relations between Blair and the US Presidency to cool. Bush was not only a Republican, but was seen as being a right-wing Republican. In so far as Europeans have negative stereotypes of Americans, Bush seemed to embody most of them. Yet Blair and Bush struck up a close relationship, and Blair became personally committed to Bush's 'war on terror'. That was so much the case that Blair was sometimes presented as being a 'poodle' to Bush. This did much damage to Blair's public profile and many critics of the war in Iraq blamed it on his obsession with maintaining strong relations with the USA.

If Iraq and Suez are rare examples of war being divisive in British politics, there is one other way in which security matters can make an impact on political debate: when civil liberties become involved. Throughout the Troubles in Northern Ireland there was extensive political scrutiny of the measures being taken to tackle paramilitary violence, in particular the use of Prevention of Terrorism Acts. The first such Act was passed in 1974 and gave the government what Home Secretary Roy Jenkins described as 'Draconian' powers of, for example, arrest and detention. Jenkins said that the powers were 'unprecedented in peace time' but added, 'I believe they are fully justified to meet the clear and present danger'.[11] The Act was regularly renewed and revised until it was replaced by the Terrorism Act of 2000, generally without significant political opposition. However, there has been more controversy in recent years over new legislation, even in the wake of the bombings in London on 7 July 2005. The 2006 Terrorism Bill, which arose from pressure for a new regime to challenge terrorism, was heavily criticised for allowing suspects to be detained for ninety days without trial, rather than the fourteen which were then law. The government was defeated on the issue and the new Act included a limit of only twenty-eight days. There were further divides within the coalition government in 2010–15 over more recent 'anti-terror' laws. Such division and such an outcome were remarkable in the post-war period at a time of 'war' and reflect what may be a growing tendency for the country not to be united over security matters.

What now?

On some levels, Britain's position in the world appears to be relatively settled. It is a member of the European Union and neither of the main parties proposes leaving the EU, even if there are elements within both which would like to do so. Membership of NATO divided the parties in the 1980s but has not been controversial since the end of the Cold War. Since 9/11, the UK has played a major role in the 'war on terror'.

However, there remain a number of issues which are controversial and could have serious effects on how Britain engages in international institutions and conflicts in the future. Britain's status as a nuclear power is under scrutiny more than ever before, with some serious attention as to whether or not the Trident system should be replaced by a similar or smaller system, or by none at all. The parliamentary debate on the bombing of Syria at the end of 2015 seriously divided Labour MPs.

Perhaps most important is Britain's relationship with America. So often dubbed a 'special relationship', it is in a state of flux. During the years of George W. Bush's presidency (2001–9), British public opinion steadily turned against the idea of American 'leadership' of the 'free world'. Yet when Barack Obama replaced Bush in early 2009, there were signs of a reassessment in Britain of America's claim to moral authority in the world. Ironically, Obama was less interested in the 'special relationship' than his predecessor. So while British politicians may find that courting the USA is more popular at home in the future than during the Bush years, it ultimately secures less influence than the relationship that Blair enjoyed with Bush.

9

Conclusion

Does British politics actually work? Of course, the answer to that depends on what one's values are and what one wants from government. There are a number of different ways of looking at the issue, but they all centre on who has political power, how they are chosen and how close they are to the voters.

There are some points on which there is broad agreement. Most people accept that the durability of the British state has been a strength of the system. There were no violent revolutions in the UK in the nineteenth or twentieth centuries even though there were times, such as the early 1920s, when people genuinely feared that public disorder might lead to a crisis. This is often attributed to the ability of Parliament to be inclusive of most demands of most people.

In the twentieth century, Parliament effectively accommodated the concerns of mainstream socialist opinion, whose advocates decided that they would pursue, in the phrase of Marxist academic Ralph Miliband, 'Parliamentary Socialism'.[1] More radical elements on both the left and the right were marginalised and attracted little public support. By and large, the public seems to have decided that it can get what it wants without all the effort of revolution, or at least that it can get enough. In enabling this situation the benefits of having an 'unwritten' constitution are cited as being that Parliament can respond quickly and easily to demands for major change. Unlike in France, if one wants to change the form of government, then constitutional change does not involve going back to rewrite basic laws. Instead, changes evolve gradually.

If the British are a little smug about this, we should perhaps reflect on a geographical factor which has contributed to stability: the English Channel. The existence of a sizeable body of water between the UK and the Continent has proved a bulwark against invasion from foreign countries. In other European countries, radical constitutional change or revolution have often been associated with, or followed on from, threats to national survival. In Britain, simply being isolated from that pressure by the Channel has meant that there have been fewer opportunities for crisis. Meanwhile, the spread of radical ideas was, to some extent, hindered by cross-channel communications, especially at the time of the French Revolution. When there has been a serious danger to Britain's survival, as in 1940, the constitution has been flexible enough to adapt to the dangers faced, with significant innovations in the system of government, which might have been less possible in a more rigid constitutional framework.

Yet aspects of the durability are hotly contested. As we saw earlier, advocates of elitist democratic theory see democracy as being about elites competing for votes and then ruling in the interests of the people. From that perspective, the British system is excellent because that is just what happens. On the other hand, those who want government to be based on the will of the majority see much wrong with the system. On this, we have to make a choice about whether we fear the coalitions which would be likely after most elections if there were a proportional voting system. Are the dangers of coalition so great as to justify maintaining the current system, or are the risks worth taking to ensure greater representation in government for a wider range of opinions?

There are also disagreements over how far radical change is possible in the UK system. Are parties all the same? Do they really want change? If they do, can they really wield power in the cause of change? We saw earlier that the period between about 1951 and about 1970 is seen as one of political consensus in which both Labour and Conservative governments pursued policies which were broadly supportive of the welfare state and government intervention in the economy. A commonly stated public view at that time was that it did not much matter which party was in power, because the policies did not change much and both parties were happy with a period of consensus. Yet radical changes did follow: there was bitter conflict between parties in the 1980s and 1990s, though many commentators now see politics organised around a neo-liberal consensus in which governments try to do as little as possible to interfere in global market forces. Some people see such continuity between governments as positive. Others are more critical, especially if they think that parties want to bring about more change but are hampered in doing so by a range of factors including the media and an intransigent civil service. Again, there are choices to be made about whether or not we think any of this is a problem. Like just about everything else in politics, it depends on your perspective.

None of this is to say that since 1945 there have not been major changes, nor that parties change little. This book has argued that, even if politics is in a state of crisis, there is little alternative than to work through political parties in order to seize control of the levers of state power. This can only be done collectively and so parties are inevitable. Moreover, this book has argued that there have been key moments since 1945 when big changes have been made. These are changes which one party would have made, but not others, and so parties clearly do make a difference.

How much change can we expect to see in the future? If radical changes are to be made then I believe that they might come in any or all of three areas: the location of political power, the environment and public spending.

When Britain is compared with other countries, one of the most striking points about political power is its location: Britain is highly centralised. That particularly applies to policy affecting England because in Wales, Northern Ireland and Scotland there is now significant devolution to national bodies. However, England is one of Europe's most centralised countries and this is clearest in one area of policy which is used as an illustration of the problem: the NHS.

As Patricia Hewitt pointed out in June 2007, 'If the NHS was a country, it would be the 33rd biggest economy in the world, larger than new European Union transition economies like Romania and Bulgaria ... The NHS is four times the size of the Cuban economy and more centralised.'[2] Within this massive bureaucracy the ability of local people to influence decisions is extremely limited. In the current system, ministers are able to claim that any local closures have followed public consultation and that decisions have been made locally. Yet the unelected bureaucrats who make such decisions pay scant attention to local wishes for two reasons. First, they do not have to: they are unelected and their jobs do not depend on any form of public satisfaction. Second, they are not able to act on most local demands because they work within tightly defined budgets and central rules, which do not allow them any flexibility in the amount of money they spend on local services.

What is the answer? Denmark offers a possible way forward. In Denmark, major powers over healthcare are given to areas of local government around the size of English counties, and the country's healthcare system is one of the most effective, and the most popular, in Europe. If such a structure can deliver a healthcare system, funded from general taxation, that is the most popular in Europe, could English cities and counties do the same?[3]

However, one problem which any attempt to devolve power in England has to deal with is that we already know that people are sceptical about schemes to establish more layers of government. Although there has been some support on the political fringes for the establishment of an English parliament, most proposals for reform in England have focused on creating regional assemblies, but these have made little headway with the public. This became clear in the referendum in the North-East of England in 2004 on the question of whether that region should have an elected regional assembly. It had been widely felt that the North-East was one of the English regions which would be most in favour of such a body yet the idea was decisively rejected. That derailed what had once looked like an unstoppable train heading towards each region of England having its own assembly.

This should not mean, however, that simply because one area of the country has voted against a specific form of devolution that it is not going to happen anywhere. While it may be the case that the regional model of government appears to have little support, future governments may well devolve power to more local levels such as counties or cities. Moreover, the Spanish system offers a model for how different powers can be devolved at different times to different parts of the same country. This is known as 'asymmetrical' devolution and has allowed those areas which want more power to have it, without waiting for others to fall in step.[4]

Changes may not only take place in where power is located, but also in how it is applied to policy. The issue which is rising fastest up the political agenda is the environment. The way in which we relate to our natural surroundings has only rarely been influential in post-war British politics. In December 1952, the people of London saw the effects of pollution when the Great Smog hit the city. As a result, as many as 12,000 may have died in just a few days.[5] Four years later, the government passed the Clean Air Act, which created urban zones where only smokeless fuels could be burnt. Between then and the 1980s, examples of concern about the environment tended to be limited to specific cases, such as the crude-oil spill from the *Torrey Canyon* tanker off the coast of Cornwall in 1967.

That is not to say that there were not people who were concerned about the environment in the broadest sense: Friends of the Earth was formed in 1971, the Ecology Party (initially just known as 'People') was formed in 1973 and became the Green Party in 1985, while the Liberal Party was concerned about environmental issues from the 1970s. But such groups and concerns were seen by most people as marginal and somewhat cranky. That began to change in September 1988 with help from an unlikely source, when Margaret Thatcher made a highly significant speech to the Royal Society. She put three issues on the agenda of mainstream politics: the greenhouse effect (which we now describe as climate change), the emergence of a hole in the ozone layer and acid rain. She went on to draw a direct link between the economy and the environment, saying:

> Stable prosperity can be achieved throughout the world provided the environment is nurtured and safeguarded. Protecting this balance of nature is therefore one of the great challenges of the late Twentieth Century.[6]

The carrying of such a message by Margaret Thatcher was ironic. The consumerist boom which Thatcher–Reagan economics encouraged was one of the major causes of the problems she raised. Yet she must also go down in history as one of the first world leaders to put the environment at the heart of the political agenda and to see it in global terms.

Since then, world leaders have made efforts to mitigate the problems that we are all causing, most notably Agenda 21, agreed at the Rio de Janeiro summit in 1992, and the Kyoto Protocol of 1997. But since such initiatives, most scientists have argued that the effects of climate change are likely to be much greater than previously imagined, and that we are not doing enough to tackle the problems. We have a limited window of opportunity in which to make a key decision from a range of possibilities. Do we take bold steps to limit climate change, do we take limited steps or do we only deal with the consequences? Some scientific evidence suggests such a bleak future that, whatever we do, we may find that the consequences are devastating. In any event, we must expect to hear much more from our politicians about climate change in the years to come.

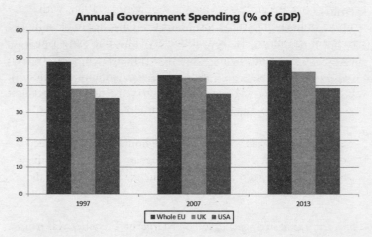

Annual Government Spending (% of GDP)

■ Whole EU   ■ UK   ■ USA

Figure 9.1[7]

In the short term, much public and political attention is likely to remain focused on the challenges facing the government budget and the long-term deficit. This will involve us as a nation determining what sort of public services we want. If we want schools and hospitals which match the best in Europe, the question is asked, are we spending enough? Or do we favour the type of small state that the USA has? The proportion of GDP spent by governments is instructive here (Figure 9.1). In 1997, the UK's level of public spending by all levels of government was far closer to that of the USA than it was to other European Union countries. Ten years later, after the New Labour government had significantly increased public spending, it was much closer to that of other EU members, at a time when EU and USA spending were broadly stable. However, in 2014, UK spending had fallen so that it was roughly midway between America and Europe. Overall, spending rose across countries as a proportion of GDP due to the economic crisis, but the UK rise mirrored that of the USA more than that of other EU members.

Governments, perhaps sometimes coalitions, will rise and fall, but fundamental challenges straddle terms of office. Europe or America, or countries far beyond? This remains one of the great questions in British politics as we determine not only with whom we wish to work on the international stage, but also what sort of society we want at home.

Notes

2 'Events, dear boy, events': a brief history of British domestic politics since 1945

1. Cited in Paul Addison, *The Road to 1945: British Politics and the Second World War* (London: Cape, 1975), p. 122.
2. For a discussion of this rivalry see: news.bbc.co.uk/1/hi/programmes/the_westminster_hour/1899102.stm (accessed 26 May 2010).
3. Kenneth Harris, *Attlee* (London: Weidenfeld & Nicolson, 1982, 1995 revised edn), p. 349.
4. See Peter Hennessy, *Having It So Good: Britain in the Fifties* (London: Allen Lane, 2006), p. 110.
5. See, in particular, Dennis Kavanagh, *Thatcherism and British Politics: the End of Consensus?* (Oxford: Oxford University Press, 1990). See also David Dutton, *British Politics Since 1945: The Rise and Fall of Consensus* (Oxford: Blackwell, 1991); Peter Hennessy and Anthony Seldon, eds, *Ruling Performance: Post-war Administrations from Attlee to Thatcher* (Oxford: Blackwell, 1987); Dennis Kavanagh, 'The Postwar Consensus', *Twentieth Century British History*, 3, 2 (1992), pp. 175–190; Rodney Lowe, 'The Second World War, Consensus, and the Foundations of the Welfare State', *Twentieth Century British History*, 1, 2 (1990), pp. 152–182; and David Marquand and Anthony Seldon, eds, *The Ideas that Shaped Post-war Britain* (London: Fontana, 1996).
6. Ben Pimlott, 'The Myth of Consensus', in *The Making of Britain: Echoes of Greatness*, L. M. Smith, ed. (London: Macmillan, 1988), pp. 129–142; Harriet Jones and Michael Kandiah, eds, *The Myth of Consensus: New Views on British History, 1945–64* (London: Macmillan, 1996).

7. For example, my own article, 'Mods, Rockers, and Juvenile Delinquency in 1964: The Government Response', in *Contemporary British History*, 12, 1 (1998), pp. 19–47.

8. An important work along these lines is Kevin Hickson, 'The Postwar Consensus Revisited', *Political Quarterly*, 75, 2 (2004), pp. 142–154.

9. *Hansard* (HC Deb 22 March 1963 vol. 674 col. 810).

10. www.margaretthatcher.org/speeches/displaydocument.asp? docid=104431 (accessed 26 May 2010).

11. Cited in Iain Dale, ed., *Labour Party General Election Manifestos, 1900–1997* (London: Routledge, 2000), p. 4.

12. Cited in Dennis Kavanagh and Anthony Seldon, *The Major Effect* (London: Macmillan, 1994), p. 9.

13. Tony Blair, 'Why Crime is a Socialist Issue', *New Statesman*, 29 January 1993, pp. 27–8.

14. www.ifs.org.uk/budgets/budget2010/browne.pdf (accessed 26 May 2010).

15. news.bbc.co.uk/1/hi/uk_politics/2120011.stm (accessed 26 May 2010).

16. *Evening Standard*, 12 May 2010, p. 21.

17. ukpollingreport.co.uk/blog/voting-intention (accessed 26 May 2010).

18. *Morning Star*, 13 May 2010, p. 1.

19. ukpollingreport.co.uk/voting-intention-2 (accessed 26 August 2015).

20. www.bbc.co.uk/news/education-11677862, www.bbc.co.uk/news/uk-politics-11952449 and https://www.youtube.com/watch?v=jTLR8R9JXz4 (accessed 26 August 2015).

21. For a full discussion, see Paul Johnson and Daniel Chandler, 'The Coalition and the Economy', in *The Coalition Effect, 2010–2015*, Anthony Seldon and Mike Finn, eds (Cambridge: Cambridge University Press, 2015), pp. 159–93.

22. www.ft.com/cms/s/0/2da09f02-cbe3-11e4-aeb5-00144feab7de.html#axzz3js5Vd8Yb (accessed 26 August 2015).

23. www.bbc.co.uk/news/events/scotland-decides/results (accessed 26 August 2015).
24. www.bbc.co.uk/news/uk politics-29271765 (accessed 26 August 2015).

3 What is British politics?

1. See A. R. Ball & B. G. Peters, *Modern Politics and Government*, 6th edn (Basingstoke: Palgrave, 2000), pp. 54–55, from which some of these points are drawn.
2. news.bbc.co.uk/1/hi/world/americas/6130302.stm (accessed 26 May 2010).
3. news.bbc.co.uk/1/hi/6975708.stm and news.bbc.co.uk/1/hi/uk_ politics/6251788.stm (accessed 26 May 2010).
4. Vernon Bogdanor, *The New British Constitution* (Oxford: Hart, 2009), p. xi.
5. Ian Budge et al., *The New British Politics*, 3rd edn (Harlow: Pearson, 2004), p. 88; Bill Jones et al., *Politics UK*, 6th edn (Harlow: Pearson, 2007), pp. 358–9; Dennis Kavanagh et al., *British Politics*, 5th edition (Oxford: Oxford University Press, 2006), pp. 179–80; Michael Moran, *Politics and Governance in the UK* (Basingstoke: Palgrave, 2005), pp. 72–6.
6. For useful summaries of the work of these writers and others, see Kavanagh et al., pp. 52–61.

4 Layer upon layer: the structure of British government

1. Cited in Ian Budge et al., *The New British Politics*, 3rd edn (Harlow: Pearson, 2004), p. 112.
2. www.independent.co.uk/news/uk/politics/blairs-kitchen-cabinet-prepares-for-rare-dose-of-public-scrutiny-536055.html (accessed 26 May 2010).
3. Cited in Geoffrey Marshall, *Constitutional Conventions: The Rules and Forms of Political Accountability* (Oxford: Clarendon Press, 1984), p. 57, n. 7.

4. www.ipsos-mori.com/researchpublications/researcharchive/poll. aspx?oItemId=122&view=wide and www.ipsos-mori.com/ researchpublications/researcharchive/poll.aspx?oItemId=114&vie w=wide (accessed 26 May 2010).
5. www.electoral-reform.org.uk/votingsystems/systems.htm (accessed 26 May 2010).
6. Michael Moran, *Politics and Governance in the UK* (Basingstoke: Palgrave, 2005), p. 266.

5 Manifestos, leaflets and members: political parties and pressure groups

1. Some of the points in this paragraph and the next are drawn from John Dearlove and Peter Saunders, *Introduction to British Politics* (Oxford: Wiley-Blackwell, 2000), pp. 90–93.
2. Michael Moran, *Politics and Governance in the UK* (Basingstoke: Palgrave, 2005), p. 286; www.telegraph.co.uk/news/newstopics/ politics/2475301/Labour-membership-falls-to-historic-low.html (accessed 26 May 2010); www.parliament.uk/briefing-papers/ SN05125.pdf (accessed 25 August 2015); www.bbc.co.uk/news/ uk-politics-33892407 (accessed 25 August 2015).
3. Conservative Party, *Invitation to Join the Government of Britain* (London: Conservative Party, 2010), p. vii; www.conservatives. com/manifesto (accessed 25 August 2015).
4. www.conservatives.com/People/Members_of_the_Board.aspx (accessed 26 May 2010).
5. Labour Party, *A Future Fair for All* (London: Labour Party, 2010), p. 3.
6. www.labour.org.uk/page/-/BritainCanBeBetter-TheLabourParty Manifesto2015.pdf (accessed 25 August 2015).
7. www.labour.org.uk/Partnership_in_power_institutions (accessed 26 May 2010).
8. www.plaidcymru.org/content.php?nID=90;lID=1 (accessed 26 May 2010).

9. www.electionpolling.co.uk/blog/2015/06/12/election-2015-
   lost-deposits (accessed 25 August 2015).
10. bnp.org.uk/policies/immigration/ (accessed 26 May 2010).
11. www.europarl.org.uk/section/european-elections/results-2009-
    european-elections-uk (accessed 26 May 2010).

6 Policy: the big issues

1. www.theguardian.com/politics/2014/jan/14/2015-uk-general-
   election-polls-analysis (accessed 27 August 2015).
2. Useful introductions to further material can be found in Roger
   Middleton, *The British Economy since 1945: Engaging with the
   Debate* (Basingstoke: Palgrave, 2000) and Nicholas Woodward,
   The Management of the British Economy, 1945–2001 (Manchester:
   Manchester University Press, 2004).
3. Office for National Statistics, 'Gross Domestic Product
   Preliminary Estimate, Quarter 2 (Apr to June) 2015', 28 July 2015,
   p. 6.
4. See, for example, https://www.gov.uk/government/speeches/
   chancellor-george-osbornes-summer-budget-2015-speech
   (accessed 27 August 2015).
5. See, OECD, General government spending at data.oecd.org/gga/
   general-government-spending.htm (accessed 14 December 2015).
6. ons.gov.uk/ons/rel/psa/public-sector-finances/july-2015/sum-
   psf-july-2015.html (accessed 27 August 2015).
7. www.ifs.org.uk/budgets/budgetjune2010/chote.pdf (accessed 27
   August 2015).
8. election2015.ifs.org.uk/public-spending (accessed 27 August
   2015).
9. Cited in Susan Crosland, *Tony Crosland* (London: Cape, 1982),
   p. 148. He only missed out schools in Scotland because there was
   a different system, over which he did not have control.
10. news.bbc.co.uk/1/hi/education/6564933.stm (accessed 28 May
    2010).

11. www.labour-party.org.uk/manifestos/1997/1997-labour-manifesto. shtml (accessed 28 May 2010).

12. Nick Clegg and Richard Grayson, *Learning from Europe: Lessons in Education* (London: Centre for European Reform, 2002).

13. Alan Smithers, 'The Coalition and Society (II): Education', in *The Coalition Effect, 2010–2015*, Anthony Seldon and Mike Finn, eds (Cambridge: Cambridge Univeristy Press, 2015), pp. 257–89 (p. 263).

14. Calculated using www.thisismoney.co.uk/historic-inflation-calculator (accessed 27 May 2010).

15. Cited in Nicholas Timmins, *The Five Giants: A Biography of the Welfare State* (London: Harper Collins, 2001), p. 101.

16. Cited in ibid., p. 203.

17. Department of Health and Social Security, *NHS Management Inquiry Report* (1983) available at www.sochealth.co.uk/history/griffiths.htm (accessed 27 May 2010).

18. www.nhs.uk/NHSEngland/thenhs/about/Pages/nhsstructure. aspx and www.gov.uk/government/organisations/monitor (accessed 27 August 2015).

19. Howard Glennerster, 'The Coalition and Society (III): Health and Long-Term Care', in *The Coalition Effect, 2010–2015*, Anthony Seldon and Mike Finn, eds (Cambridge: Cambridge University Press, 2015), pp. 290–316).

20. Soumaya Keynes and Gemma Tetlow, *Survey of Public Spending in the UK* (London: Institute for Fiscal Studies, 2014), pp. 11 and 16.

21. www.independent.co.uk/news/uk/politics/labours-record-on-poverty-in-tatters-1681047.html (8 May 2009, accessed 27 May 2010).

22. www.un-documents.net/wced-ocf.htm (accessed 28 May 2010).

23. HM Government, *Securing the Future: Delivering UK Sustainable Development Strategy* (The Stationery Office, 2005); HM Government, *Climate Change: The UK Programme* (The Stationery Office, 2006); Joint Nature Conservation Committee & Department for Environment, Food and Rural Affairs, *The UK Post-2010 Biodiversity Framework* (JNCC & DEFRA, 2012).

24. Department for Work and Pensions, *The Single-tier Pension: A Simple Foundation for Saving* (Norwich: The Stationery Office, 2013).

25. www.bbc.co.uk/news/business-33009399 (accessed 27 August 2015).

26. www.theguardian.com/environment/2010/oct/13/europe-kyoto-targets-emissions (accessed 27 August 2015).

27. www.businessgreen.com/bg/news/2405701/davey-this-has-been-the-greenest-government-ever and www.theguardian.com/environment/2015/mar/12/did-coalition-live-up-to-greenest-government-pledge (accessed 27 August 2015).

7 Power without responsibility: the media

1. Cited in James Curran and Jean Seaton, *Power without Responsibility: The Press and Broadcasting in Britain* (London: Routledge, 1997), p. 42.

2. media.guardian.co.uk/presspublishing/tables/0,,632628,00.html; www.guardian.co.uk/media/table/2010/mar/12/abcs-dailies-february-2010 (accessed 27 May 2010) and www.pressgazette.co.uk/national-newspaper-abcs-july-2015-queen-and-lord-sewel-help-sun-strong-month-month-performance (accessed 25 August 2015).

3. www.conservatives.com/Video/Webcameron.aspx; http://iaindale.blogspot.com/; order-order.com/; and www.theliberati.net/quaequamblog/ (accessed 27 May 2010).

4. yatterbox.com/blog/2015/05/record-number-of-mps-now-using-twitter-2/ (accessed 25 August 2015).

5. www.telegraph.co.uk/news/general-election-2015/politics-blog/11590772/Who-won-the-Twitter-campaign-battle.html (accessed 4 October 2015).

6. www.theguardian.com/politics/2014/mar/06/politicians-twitter-top-5-gaffes-cameron-phone-obama (accessed 4 October 2015).

7. Michael Moran, *Politics and Governance in the UK* (Basingstoke: Palgrave, 2005), pp. 358–9; Ian Budge et al., *The New British Politics*, 3rd edn (Harlow: Pearson, 2004), pp. 339–43; Bill Jones et al., *Politics UK*, 6th edn (Harlow: Pearson, 2007), p. 232.

8. news.bbc.co.uk/onthisday/hi/correspondents/newsid_2626000/2626349.stm (accessed 26 May 2010).

9. Moran, p. 358.

10. The *Sun*, 9 April 1992, p. 1.

11. news.bbc.co.uk/1/hi/uk_politics/6744581.stm (accessed 27 May 2010).

12. www.bbc.co.uk/blogs/newsnight/2007/08/the_james_mactaggart_memorial_lecture.html and www.bbc.co.uk/blogs/nickrobinson/2006/01/marital_problem.html (both accessed 28 May 2010).

13. Andrew Marr, *My Trade: A Short History of British Journalism* (Macmillan: London, 2004), pp. 63 and 188.

14. news.bbc.co.uk/1/hi/uk_politics/6744581.stm (accessed 27 May 2010).

15. Cited in Steven Clayman and John Heritage, *The News Interview: Journalists and Public Figures on the Air* (Cambridge: Cambridge University Press, 2002), pp. 189–90.

8 Losing an Empire, finding a role: British politics and the wider world

1. Richard English and Michael Kenny, 'Conclusion: Decline or Declinism?', in *Rethinking British Decline*, Richard English and Michael Kenny, eds (London: Macmillan, 2000), pp. 279–99.

2. *Hansard* (HC Deb 12 June 1979 vol. 968 col. 237).

3. Adam Smith, *An Inquiry into the Nature and Causes of the Wealth of Nations* (London: Adam and Charles Black, 1863, originally published 1776), p. 152.

4. *The Times*, 4 November 1902, p. 5.

5. www.conservativemanifesto.com/1987/1987-conservative-manifesto.shtml (accessed 27 May 2010).

6. Nicolas Crafts and Gianni Toniolo, *Economic Growth in Europe since 1945* (Cambridge: Cambridge University Press, 1996), p. 6; *OECD Factbook 2009: Economic, Environmental and Social Statistics* (OECD, 2009).

7. See, for example, Ronald Hyam, 'Bureaucracy and "Trusteeship" in the Colonial Empire', *The Oxford History of the British Empire, Vol. IV: The Twentieth Century*, Judith M. Brown and Wm. Roger Louis, eds (Oxford: Oxford University Press, 1999), pp. 255–79.

8. www.margaretthatcher.org/speeches/displaydocument.asp?docid=107332 (accessed 27 May 2010).

9. www.armedforces.co.uk/mod/listings/l0021.html (accessed 15 January 2016).

10. www.bbc.co.uk/worldservice/history/story/2007/01/070124_suez.shtml (accessed 27 May 2010).

11. *Hansard* (HC Deb 25 November 1974 vol. 882 col. 35).

9 Conclusion

1. Ralph Miliband, *Parliamentary Socialism: A Study in the Politics of Labour* (London: George Allen and Unwin, 1961).

2. Patricia Hewitt, 'The NHS: The Next Ten Years', Speech at London School of Economics, 14 June 2007 at www.lse.ac.uk/collections/LSEPublicLecturesAndEvents/pdf/20070614_Hewitt.pdf (accessed 29 June 2009).

3. Richard S. Grayson, 'Reforming the NHS: A Local and Democratic Voice', in *Reinventing the State: Social Liberalism for the 21st Century*, Duncan Brack, Richard S. Grayson and David Howarth, eds (London: Politicos, 2007), pp. 269–86.

4. Luis Moreno, 'Decentralization in Spain', *Regional Studies*, 36, 4 (2002), pp. 399–408, at http://www.iesam.csic.es/doctrab2/dt-0115.pdf (accessed 27 May 2010).

5. news.bbc.co.uk/1/hi/health/2545747.stm (accessed 27 May 2010).

6. www.margaretthatcher.org/speeches/displaydocument. asp?docid=107346 (accessed 27 May 2010).

7. Figure 9.1 data comes from the OECD, General government spending at https://data.oecd.org/gga/general-government-spending.htm (accessed 14 December 2015). Note that the OECD does not have data on all EU members. For example, there is no data on Greece, nor for some former members of the Soviet Union.

Further reading

General textbooks, analyses or collections

The following textbooks cover in greater depth many of the issues raised in this book:

Budge, I. et al. 2007, 4th edition. *The New British Politics*. Harlow: Pearson.

Jones, B. et al. 2011, 8th edition. *Politics UK*. London: Routledge.

Kavanagh, D. et al. 2006, 5th edition. *British Politics*. Oxford: Oxford University Press.

Moran, M. 2015, 3rd edition. *Politics and Governance in the UK*. Basingstoke: Palgrave.

Some general themes covering British politics since 1945 are tackled in:

Darwin, J. 2006. *The End of the British Empire: The Historical Debate*. Oxford: Wiley-Blackwell.

Hickson, K., 'The Postwar Consensus Revisited', *Political Quarterly*, 75, 2 (2004), pp. 142–54.

Kavanagh, D. 1990. *Thatcherism and British Politics: The End of Consensus?* Oxford: Oxford University Press.

Kavanagh, D. 1997. *The Reordering of British Politics after Thatcher*. Oxford: Oxford University Press.

Marquand, D. and Seldon, A. eds. 1996. *The Ideas that Shaped Post-war Britain*. London: Fontana.

A regularly updated series of studies looks at current developments and the most recent is:

Dunleavy, P. et al. eds. 2006. *Developments in British Politics 8.* Basingstoke: Palgrave.

Issues around elections are covered in another series, covering each election since 1945, the most recent of which is:

Butler, D. and Cowling, P. 2015. *The British General Election of 2015.* Basingstoke: Palgrave.

Structure of government

The following cover issues around the structure of government and constitutional matters:

Bogdanor, V. 2001. *Devolution in the United Kingdom.* Oxford: Oxford University Press.
Bogdanor, V. ed. 2004. *The British Constitution in the Twentieth Century.* Oxford: Oxford University Press.
Bogdanor, V. 2009. *The New British Constitution.* Oxford: Hart.
Judge, D. 2005. *Political Institutions in the United Kingdom.* Oxford: Oxford University Press.

Parties and pressure groups

Issues affecting political parties and pressure groups are tackled in:

Grant, W. 2000. *Pressure Groups and British Politics.* Basingstoke: Palgrave.
Lovenduski, J. 2005. *Feminizing Politics.* Cambridge: Polity.
Webb. P. 2000. *The Modern British Party System.* London: Sage.

Specific parties are considered in:

Charmley, J. 2008. *A History of Conservative Politics since 1830.* Basingstoke: Palgrave.

D'Ancona, M. 2013. *In it Together: The Inside Story of the Coalition*. London: Viking.

Dutton, D. 2004. *A History of the Liberal Party in the Twentieth Century*. Basingstoke: Palgrave.

Garnett, M. and Lynch, P. eds. 2003. *The Conservatives in Crisis: The Tories after 1997*. Manchester: Manchester University Press.

Gould, P. 1999. *The Unfinished Revolution: How Modernisers saved the Labour Party*. London: Abacus.

Pelling, H. and Reid, A. J. 2005, 12th edition. *A Short History of the Labour Party*. Basingstoke: Palgrave.

Rawnsley, A. 2001. *Servants of the People: The Inside Story of New Labour*. London: Penguin.

Russell, A. and Fieldhouse, E. 2004. *Neither Left nor Right? The Electoral Politics of the Liberal Democrats*. Manchester: Manchester University Press.

Media

The best introduction to the media's role in politics is:

Curran, J. and Seaton, J. 2009, 7th edition. *Power without Responsibility: The Press, Broadcasting and New Media in Britain*. London: Routledge.

Political histories and policy

There are countless books dealing with the political history of post-1945 British politics. A useful starting point is:

Morgan, Kenneth O. 2001. *Britain since 1945: The People's Peace*. Oxford: Oxford University Press.

A valuable survey of the devastating nature of the Troubles in Northern Ireland is:

McKittrick, D. and McVea, D. 2001. *Making Sense of the Troubles*. London: Penguin.

Excellent assessments of recent policy are:

Seldon, A. ed. 2007. *Blair's Britain, 1997–2007*. Cambridge: Cambridge University Press.
Seldon, A. and Finn, M. eds. 2015. *The Coalition Effect, 2010–2015*. Cambridge, Cambridge University Press.

Index